HENRY SALT

HENRY SALT

Humanitarian Reformer and Man of Letters

GEORGE HENDRICK

with the special assistance of John F. Pontin

UNIVERSITY OF ILLINOIS PRESS

Urbana   Chicago   London

Letters of George Bernard Shaw dated Sept. 27, 1910; Sept. 14, 1926; Oct. 3, 1926; and Jan. 13, 1928, are quoted courtesy of the Humanities Research Center, University of Texas at Austin; and the Henry W. and Albert A. Berg Collection, The New York Public Library, Astor, Lenox and Tilden Foundation. © 1977 The Trustees of the British Museum, The Governors and Guardians of the National Gallery of Ireland and the Royal Academy of Dramatic Art.

LIBRARY OF CONGRESS CATALOGING IN PUBLICATION DATA

Hendrick, George.
　　Henry Salt, humanitarian reformer and man of
letters.

　Includes bibliographical references and index.
　1. Salt, Henry Stephens, 1851–1939.　2. Authors,
English—19th century—Biography.
PR5299.S217Z7　　　823'.9'12　　　77-5142
ISBN 0-252-00611-9

FOR SARAH

Acknowledgments

While the writing of this study is all mine, I am particularly indebted to John F. Pontin of Manchester, England; he generously provided me with materials from his Salt collection, answered my many questions, and read and commented on the manuscript. Without his help this study could not have been written.

For permission to quote from manuscripts and letters, I am indebted to the Gandhi National Museum and Library, New Delhi; the British Library, London; the Henry W. and Albert A. Berg Collection of the New York Public Library; the Houghton Library, Harvard University, Cambridge, Massachusetts; the Sheffield City Libraries, Sheffield, England; the Humanities Research Center, University of Texas at Austin; the University of Illinois Library at Urbana-Champaign; the Society of Authors and the Trustees of the British Museum, the Governors and Guardians of the National Gallery of Ireland and the Royal Academy of Dramatic Art on behalf of the Bernard Shaw estate; the late Mrs. P. V. B. Jones; John F. Pontin; and Catherine Mandeville Salt.

I am also indebted to the Research Board of the University of Illinois for funds which allowed me to purchase microfilm of nineteenth-century periodicals to which Salt made contributions and to the Center for Advanced Study at the University of Illinois, where I spent eight months as an associate member and completed the research and writing of this study.

George Hendrick

Contents

Introduction

"I SHALL DIE, AS I HAVE LIVED, A RATIONALIST,
SOCIALIST, PACIFIST AND HUMANITARIAN"

When Henry S. Salt died in Brighton, England, on April 19, 1939, the address that he had written for the burial service was read by his friend Bertram Lloyd and published five days later in the *Sussex Daily News*. Lloyd, who began the service by noting that Salt was known to an earlier generation as humanitarian, socialist, and freethinker, emphasized the fact that his rebellion against conventional ideas had not faded in his old age, and concluded with Salt's statement:

Friends: It is not usual, I think, for a funeral address to have been written in anticipation, and by the person who has died; but I ask you in this case to excuse the arrangement as one that is likely to save trouble to somebody, and give the deceased the assurance that the words said at his cremation will be what he himself would have desired. He promises, in return, to be brief.

Names are very liable to be misunderstood; and when I say that I shall die, as I have lived, a rationalist, socialist, pacifist and humanitarian, I must make my meaning clear. I wholly disbelieve in the present established religion; but I have a very firm religious faith of my own—a Creed of Kinship, I call it—a belief that in years yet to come there will be a recognition of the brotherhood

I

between man and man, nation and nation, human and sub-human, which will transform a state of semi-savagery, as we have it, into one of civilization, when there will be no such barbarity as warfare, or the robbery of the poor by the rich, or the ill-usage of the lower animals by mankind.

Such is my faith; and it is because I hold all supernatural doctrines taught under the name of religion to be actually harmful, in diverting attention from the real truths, that I believe them to have a tendency, as Ingersoll expressed it, to "petrify the human heart."

But love and friendship are fortunately quite independent of creeds, and in this farewell I would say a word of deep gratitude for the wonderful kindness that I have met with throughout life, whether from the comparatively few who have been in close agreement with my thoughts, or some of the many who have dissented from them. Of the personal love that has been my portion I will not attempt to speak.

In the funeral address, Salt touched on the main concerns of his life. It is clear, even to those who have never before heard of Salt, that he was an extraordinary man whose humane views could only have clashed with the established dogmas of his own age.

The London obituaries recognized his unique qualities, but they appeared too soon after his death to contain the funeral statement he had written, though they did summarize his life in some detail, in many cases emphasizing his devotion to a multitude of causes. *The Daily Telegraph* obituary of April 20, 1939, contained this opening paragraph: "Mr. Henry Stephens Salt, one of the great characters of his time, and probably the oldest surviving Eton master, died at his home in Brighton yesterday at the age of 87. He was a classical scholar, a wit, and the author of many books, and he took delight in having been regarded as the most thorough-going faddist in Britain."

The Times published a lengthy story that same day, quoting extensively from Salt's autobiographies, attempting to explain his conversion from Eton master to reformer:

He was born in India in 1851, the son of Colonel T. H. Salt, of the Royal Bengal Artillery, and went to Eton, then under the rule of Hornby, and thence to King's, Cambridge, where he won Sir William Browne's medal for a Greek epigram and was bracketed with Gerald Balfour as 5th classic in the Tripos of 1875. He then returned to Eton as a master and remained there in that capacity until 1884. Meanwhile in 1879 he married Catherine Leigh Joynes, a daughter of a fellow-master, the Rev. J. L. Joynes. Mrs. Salt died in 1919; and in 1927 he married Catherine, daughter of Frederick Mandeville, of Brighton.

As he himself has related, it was not long before he began to view the world differently from his colleagues; he became acquainted with men and doctrines quite foreign to the circle in which Hornby and Warre [headmasters at Eton] moved, and the conviction came upon him that the Eton masters "were but cannibals in cap and gown." He accordingly renounced flesh food, and feeling himself more and more to be living *in partibus infidelium* he resigned his mastership. Warre attributed his conduct to vegetarianism, but on learning that Socialism was also to blame cried in hearty tones: —"Socialism! Then blow us up, blow us up. There's nothing left for it but that!" Though Salt did not blow Eton up, he criticized the system as he knew it under Hornby with some freedom in articles soon afterwards.

On leaving Eton he settled in Surrey, where he pursued a simple and servantless life, which was congenial to him, gardening, writing, and getting into touch with a variety of men whose opinions were more or less in accordance with his own. He read and admired a good deal of current revolutionary literature; attended diligently the doings of the Shelley Society of which F. J. Furnivall was the leading spirit; got to know Meredith and Swinburne and other leaders of his time, and published books on Shelley, Tennyson, Thoreau, Jefferies, and James Thomson. Lucretius he always admired, and he translated in verse some of his finest passages.

In 1891 the Humanitarian League, which was to promote under the general direction of Salt all the causes which he had at heart, was founded; and Salt directed it until it ceased to exist in 1920. From his office in Chancery Lane he proved himself a good-tempered but thoroughly resourceful agitator and antagonist, who could conduct a campaign against flesh-eating, or blood sports, or the vulgarization of scenery—wild flowers, he held, should be visited, not picked—or the keeping of wild animals in captivity, or the crueller aspects of the criminal law, without losing his temper even when the fortune of war least favoured him.

As a reformer he was happily gifted with a sense of humour and the power of seeing his opponent's point of view; but these qualities did not detract from his sincerity. As his "Seventy Years Among Savages" shows, he could testify to a good many improvements in his lifetime, and "savages" as his fellowmen were, he admitted that he had found most of them to be kindly savages. When his league came to an end he uttered no unmanly lament and was under no illusions about the unpopularity of the opinions which he had endeavoured to advance.

Several of the obituaries, without giving details, noted Salt's friendship with George Bernard Shaw, William Morris, George Meredith, M. K. Gandhi, and many other writers and reformers who began their careers in the late Victorian period.

Though the death notices were generally accurate in their facts, and all sympathetic in their presentations, not one suggested the complexity of the man and his ideas. After his death, until 1951 when Stephen Winsten's *Salt and His Circle* appeared, Salt was almost forgotten. His autobiographies, *Seventy Years Among Savages* and *Company I Have Kept,* were infrequently quoted during those years; his books, which had never sold well, were no longer available; and his humanitarian and pacifist views were hardly popular during the Second World War and the Cold War which was to follow. Winsten's book did make Salt known again, but it was discursive and anecdotal, largely ignoring Salt's intellectual life and his work as social and literary critic. Worse, Winsten filled his book with reconstructed conversations which were often more fictional than historical. John Davies, in his review of the book in the *Vegetarian Messenger,* noted that Shaw's memory was failing when he wrote the preface to *Salt and His Circle,* and though the preface is "delightfully Shavian it is wildly incorrect as regards facts and mischievous as regards choice of points for emphasis."[1]

This study will go beyond the basic biographical facts given in the obituaries quoted above to concentrate on Salt's conventional youth and his conversion to vegetarianism, socialism and other "isms." Salt will be allowed to speak again for himself from the pages of several radical publications of the 1880s and 1890s, as well as from two of his own publications—*Humanity* (later called *The Humanitarian*) and *The Humane Review*—in which he opposed infliction of avoidable suffering "on any sentient being," wrote against sports based on the suffering or slaughter of animals, attacked the feather and fur trade, supported prison reform and better treatment of subjected races in the colonies, and propagandized for many other causes, such as vegetarianism and antivivisection. His two one-act propaganda plays will be reprinted in their entirety.

Salt was also a man of letters and literary critic, and his interpretations of the ideas of Shelley, Thoreau, De Quincey, and other literary figures whose works he admired, and one—Lord Tennyson—whose work he strongly attacked, will be presented. His devoted work on Thoreau, and the Thoreau-Salt-Gandhi ties, will be explored, as well as the tangled personal relationships of the Salts, Edward Carpenter, and the Shaws.

In the last year of his life, Shaw wrote, "My pastime has been writing sermons in plays, sermons preaching what Salt practised. Salt was original and in his way unique."[2] It is the originality and uniqueness of Henry Salt the humanitarian which will be emphasized in the chapters to follow.

NOTES

1. From an undated review in the Pontin/Salt collection, Manchester, England.

2. Bernard Shaw, preface to Stephen Winsten's *Salt and His Circle* (London: Hutchinson, 1951), p. 14.

1

Henry Salt: Respectable

> Respectables are we,
> And you presently shall see
> Why we confidently claim to be respected;
> In well-ordered homes we dwell
> And discharge our duties well
> Well dressed, well fed, well mannered, well connected.
>
> "Song of the Respectables,"
> *Salt and His Circle*

Henry Salt was a man of many causes, and in order to emphasize these causes, he deliberately suppressed his own inner life when he wrote his autobiographies, *Seventy Years Among Savages* (1921), *Memories of Bygone Eton* (1928), and *Company I Have Kept* (1930). These volumes are valuable for social history and for analyses of the movements in which Salt and the reformers of his age were involved, but they are vague about Salt the man.

Born in India in 1851, Salt was returned to England at the age of one, following a four-month voyage around the Cape of Good Hope. He spent a happy childhood in Shrewsbury, but, according to Shaw, disliked his father, who was an officer in the Royal Bengal Artillery, and who, Salt believed, had mistreated Henry's mother.[1] Shaw apparently had first-hand evidence for his opinion of Salt's attitude toward his parents;

his impression was also shared by John Davies, another close friend of Henry Salt. Salt's surviving letters and the brief diary of Mrs. E. M. Salt, Henry's mother, do not give any overt indications of strained relations between the elder Salts. The diary does show, however, that Mrs. Salt and Henry lived in England, that Colonel Salt remained on duty in India, and that there were infrequent reunions.[2]

Part of Salt's childhood was spent in the home of his maternal grandfather, C. B. Allnatt, a Shrewsbury barrister. Grandfather Allnatt was "shy," "sensitive," and "whimsical," qualities inherited by his grandson. A proper, upper-middle class family, it also contained its share of eccentrics to enliven young Salt's life. One uncle had a great fear of being buried prematurely and offered to make Salt his heir, on the condition that Salt would personally see that the uncle's head was severed before burial. Salt wrote years later, "This proposal I unwisely declined, from an over-conscientious doubt whether I should be able to carry such instructions into effect; and the property accordingly passed into the hands of some cousins who presumably undertook to complete the desired severance, and I trust did so."[3] This same Allnatt uncle was interested in genealogy, tracing the family ancestry to King Frederick I of Denmark. Perhaps knowledge of his royal blood helped confirm Henry Salt in the serene pursuit of his own causes. At any rate, he used his royal background for comic purposes in his poem "The Modern Ethelred (Ancestry of the Author)":

> A Saxon prince I reigned on earth;
> "The Unready" was my name:
> Less glorious is my second birth;
> Less gay my later fame.

For sceptre, pen; for castle, cot;
For crown, mere cap on head:
I'm Author now, not King, and not
The Unready, but the Unread. [4]

Though his royal blood was foreign, he had well-known English relatives; his paternal grandmother was the sister of John Moultrie. Moultrie is now largely forgotten as a poet, but in the nineteenth century he enjoyed a considerable literary reputation. [5]

Salt's aunt, Emily Allnatt, married the Reverend Edward Polehampton, chaplain at Lucknow. During the Mutiny, she was widely praised for her care of the sick and wounded. After the death of her first husband, she married Sir Henry Durand, governor of the North-Western Provinces. Sir Henry's son Mortimer, later to be ambassador in Washington, was a schoolmate of Henry's at Blackheath Proprietary School.

Salt's paternal grandfather also lived in Shrewsbury; he was a staid banker who did not encourage small boys to be familiar. He was not, it is clear, an influence upon young Salt, who was in all ways more influenced by his mother and her relatives than by his father and his paternal relatives. [6]

Salt's childhood was that of the well-to-do and socially accepted, and he made valuable friends even as a schoolboy. He was sent to the Reverend C. Kegan Paul at Sturminster Marshall in Dorsetshire for coaching for Eton. A radical minister and former chaplain at Eton, Paul later became a London publisher and was of great help to Salt and other socialists. Paul prepared Salt for confirmation and asked only one question at the rites, "Is it wrong to doubt?" Salt's "No" was the correct answer. [7] In years to come, Salt was to doubt all established religions and creeds.

Eton and Cambridge

Upon admittance to Eton as a King's Scholar, Salt entered into the happiest period of his life. For twenty years Eton was to be the focus of his activities; he was to make lasting friendships there, to marry, and to be charmed away by vegetarianism, socialism, and a Thoreauvian Simple Life. Though he was later to turn against Eton's educational philosophy and its catering to the privileged, he would not deny its early hold upon him. In *Seventy Years Among Savages* he wrote, ". . . as Eton never really changes, it is best to regard her . . . in a mood of good-natured unconcern, and as a subject less for argument than for anecdote."

Dr. J. J. Hornby became headmaster soon after Salt arrived at Eton, and Salt was later to fault him for being too weak for the position and for allowing the slackness which characterized the intellectual life of the institution. Discipline was nonexistent, and the schoolboy Salt threw himself into the "heedless existence" of the school.[8] Not burdened by arduous studies, Salt found it a time for great friendships; throughout his life he continued to cultivate his gift for making friends. Unlike some other reformers, Salt had a strong interest in people, and his causes did not make him dehumanize people. He disliked much of what went on in the world, but he did not hate those whose views were different from his own; he tried to change ways of thinking and he often liked his adversaries, seeing their foibles and yet remaining their friends.

Eton boys had their breakfast and tea in their studies, and generally several kindred spirits gathered twice a day. "The joys of this companionship," Salt says in *Memories of Bygone Eton*, "were manifold; it was a family, a party, a club, and a debating society all in one."[9] Even during his student days he was a good listener and observer, one who could phrase an excellent retort and could describe, with ironic delight, the scene around him.

Friendships in all-male Eton were often homosexual, but Salt only hints in one place of being drawn into the homosexual world of the college. In *Company I Have Kept,* he says that when he left for Cambridge, his parting with his friend Arthur Ryle "was of a quite tender kind."[10] In writing about William Johnson, author of *Ionica,* who was sent away from Eton after a homosexual scandal, Salt remarked that the problem needed to be faced instead of evaded. This statement is in keeping with his humane views and not an indication of his own sexual preferences.

C. Kegan Paul, in his *Memories,* spoke of the Eton of a few years before Salt enrolled in terms of "bullying, discomfort, and misery."[11] Salt's account in no way belies that assessment. It is fortunate that he was able to make friends, for he makes it clear that the college was almost completely unintellectual, that athletics was venerated above all else, and that years in school were a disservice to the gaining of knowledge. This mature view of his is quite similar to Thoreau's views on education at Harvard.

That Salt could have seen the grave faults of the educational system at Eton and yet have recalled it with great affection gives an indication of his ability to accept those things which he could not change. It is also an expression of his appreciation for the bonds of human friendship which he always found important.

Though Salt came to disbelieve in the Eton educational system, he valued his Eton friendships. After fifty years, he wrote that he could meet again a schoolfellow and that they could resume their "acquaintance on the former footing as easily as if we had been next door neighbors all the time."[12] For all his socialist views, Salt did not turn against the "old boy network," but recognized it for what it was. The conclusion to *Eton under Hornby* states the case succinctly: "It is easy to tinker with external forms and institutions: to change the inner immemorial spirit of a school—a school of well-bred boys who are under no real compulsion to work—is a difficult, perhaps insuperable task. Not, I think, till rich men become less rich, will rich men's sons become less idle. Till then the lordship of brawn over brain will continue at Eton as in Hornby's days, and boys will still feel that 'where ignorance is bliss, 'tis folly to be wise.' "[13]

Salt left Eton for Cambridge, but he was not happy at King's College, where he found much "ancient pettiness."[14] Undergraduates attended lectures and chapel services; the lectures were tedious, the sermons trying. Salt read conscientiously for the Classical Tripos and did not denigrate the intellectual benefits of intensive study, but he found, as a mature man writing his memoirs, that the chief fault of his university training had been the almost complete lack of concern for "the higher social ethics." It was his belief that "the weightiest charge against the University education is the one which least often finds expression—that a learning which would strengthen the intellect only, and does not feed the heart, is in the main but barren and unprofitable, a culture of the *literæ inhumaniores*."[15]

Salt remembered his Cambridge days as the least interesting in his life, for he spent most of his time "cramming." For honors, he had a first class in the Classical Tripos of 1875, and, at the age of 24, he found himself invited back to Eton as an assistant master. His prospects were excellent—respectability, the affluent life—but, after a few years, Salt was to change radically; he was to see the world in almost completely different ways.

Eton Again

Once the appointment to Eton had been made, Salt observed in *Seventy Years Among Savages,* Dr. Hornby seemed no longer interested in Salt or the problems the new master was to face. There were more teachers than suitable rooms, and most often the novice Eton master was given "The Dog-Kennel" under the stairwell, a room completely unsuited for educational purposes. Worse, the new masters had no guidance and were generally ill-equipped to instruct young students.

Only a few of the boys were interested in intellectual matters, Salt noted dryly:

New ideas were under a ban at Eton; notwithstanding the specious invitations given to some distinguished men to lecture before the school. Gladstone, Arnold, Ruskin, Morris and Lowell were among those who addressed the boys in the School Library; and it was instructive to note the reception which they severally obtained. Lowell was the most popular; his cheery contention that this world of ours is, after all, "not a bad world to live in," being delightedly received by an audience which had good personal reasons for concurring in such a sentiment: William Morris, on the other hand, having ventured on the then dangerous ground of Socialism, was hissed. Gladstone discreetly kept to the unimpeachable subject of Homer; and Matthew Arnold's staid appearance, with his "mutton-chop" whiskers and mechanical bowing of the head in accord with the slow rhythm of his sentences, was sufficient to lull to sleep any insidious doubts of his respectability. As a speaker, Ruskin was by far superior to the rest; his lucid train of thought and clear, musical voice could hold enchanted an audience, even of Eton boys, for the full space of an hour.[16]

Science, Salt complained, was hardly taken seriously, but the outer forms of organized religion were, though the tone of the college was distinctly worldly. The numerous sermons were dull and tedious; in his twenty years at Eton and Cambridge, he spent thousands of hours in chapel, enough reason alone to drive him to rationalism. Instead of ethical training, Eton stressed bookish theology, with no appreciable influence on most students.

The real creed at Eton, Salt came to believe, was Respectability. Form was more important than content. To follow the narrow conventions of society was expected. Henry Salt seemed to be completely Respectable, but after a few years as a junior master he began to change. In 1879 he married, according to the Rites and Ceremonies of the Church of England, Catherine Leigh Joynes, daughter of the Reverend J. L. Joynes, Sr., Lower Master at Eton, and sister of his friend J. L. Joynes, Jr., who had been a fellow student at Cambridge and who had also returned to Eton as a junior master. Edward Carpenter, who met the Salts in the middle 1880s, described Kate in *My Days and Dreams* as "dark, raven-haired, with large eyes and sensitive, somewhat sad, Dante-like profile. . . . She was intensely emotional, too emotional, but—as such people often are—highly musical; and her literary gift was certainly one of the most remarkable I have known—though unfortunately except in her letters, rarely utilized."[17]

Shaw, in his preface to *Salt and His Circle,* maintained that the tragedy of Salt's life was that Kate was a lesbian and would not consummate the marriage. Confirmation of Shaw's statement is not possible from Salt's own published works— but is possible from a letter in the Edward Carpenter papers. Kate wrote Carpenter in 1901, ". . . we two poor things [she and Henry] dwelling here together like friendly strangers— no touch possible (oh! the pity of it!) and no understanding. But 20 years bring deep chains that could never be cut through. . . ." Kate, after saying she and Henry were bound together, went on to confess that only recently had she realized what the unconventional marriage had done to Henry. Her realization came after she had gone with her lover Mary to Windermere. When Henry joined them a week later, Mary went to another house to sleep, for there was not enough room for all of them in the same house. "I had the most awful moment of *awakening,*" Kate wrote, "that I've ever known in my life. I had never before realized *what* I had done in letting myself get married. At the same time, such profound *Pity* took hold of me, seeing as for the first time what I had done to *him* by marrying him, that I believe he was safe from that moment—I mean I could never have thought again of deserting him—poor lonely thing."[18] After her death, Salt and Carpenter destroyed most of the letters, but this revealing letter somehow survived.

Shaw says that Kate called herself an Urning, taking the term from Carpenter.[19] Shaw maintains further, in the preface to *Salt and His Circle,* that Carpenter taught Kate that Urnings were a chosen race. From his comments it is clear that when Shaw knew the Salts and Carpenter, her sexual preferences were discussed and that Carpenter supported her sexual views. Shaw's revelation of Kate's refusal to consummate the marriage was made in a rather brusque way in the preface, perhaps partly in self-protection, since there are many indications that Shaw's life-long marriage to Charlotte Payne-Townshend was not consummated.[20] Was Shaw afraid to admit that Mrs. Shaw's fear of sex was the tragedy of his life? Did Shaw begin by admiring the Salts' companionate marriage, only to find that in his own case such a marriage was less than perfect, or was Shaw being devilish and provocative, as he revealed the bedroom secrets of a respected socialist and humanitarian? Was Henry Salt aware of Kate's sexual views before their marriage? There is no evidence now available to answer any of these questions. Salt seemingly accepted all sexual attitudes and activities without making moral judgments.

SOCIALISM AND VEGETARIANISM

Salt had begun to be aware of social issues, and during the winter holidays of 1878–79 he met William Harrison Riley, a communist. Their conversations opened another world for Salt. Through Riley, who lived at St. George's Farm, which Ruskin owned, Salt met Ruskin at a luncheon. Ruskin expressed doubts about Tennyson, attacking the hero in "Maud" as "an ass and fool" and characterizing the warlike spirit of the poem as "downright mischievous." The attacks on Tennyson, Salt says, "sapped the simple faith of an Eton master."[21]

Salt also became a rationalist at this time. The Rev. C. Kegan Paul had earlier encouraged him to doubt, and Salt had himself been bored by thousands of religious services. He ended a poem, "The Joy That Never Palls," with these lines which show his disenchantment with organized religion:

> In grave procession to the house of prayer
>   The pious people flock, demurely drest;
> Nor need'st thou ask if I myself be there
>   On this, the day of rest.
>
> Lest others tread the paths where pleasure calls:
>   For trivial, worldly joys let others search;
> To me, the bliss divine that never palls
>   Is—not to go to church![22]

Probably the great influence on Salt's religious views was Shelley. In Shelley's essay on atheism and in his poetry, Salt clearly found an intellectual basis for his rationalism.

In addition, largely through his brother-in-law J. L. Joynes, Jr., Salt began to meet the more active social reformers of the day. About 1880, Joynes met Shaw in London and soon brought him to Eton to meet the Salts. An intimate friendship began and was to last until Shaw's marriage in 1898, after which Kate was excluded, or excluded herself. Charlotte Shaw seemingly attempted to cut Shaw off from some of his old friends, but the second Mrs. Salt quoted her husband's view that it was Kate who had ended the close friendship.[23] The Shaw-Salt friendship continued on a less intimate basis until Salt's death. Salt and Shaw were to disagree during the Boer War on socialist support of the war, but their differences did not bring about a rupture of their friendship.

Salt at this time was also coming under the influence of

vegetarianism, an "ism" which was particularly suspect since "it had to be practised as well as preached." This dangerous doctrine (most Etonians were as amazed as Concordians were who heard that Thoreau ate no meat) had also been advocated by Shelley in "Queen Mab" and in various pamphlets. At this time, too, Howard Williams's classic in the field, *Ethics of Diet,* was first appearing serially. Salt thought Williams's book "of rare merit."[24] The first edition, published in 1883, contained a preface which set forth the arguments in favor of vegetarianism, followed by fifty studies of dietetic reformers, from Hesiod to Schopenhauer. It was a scholarly history, clearly marked by Williams's own compassion and concern for all sentient beings. The individual studies concentrated on the moral and ethical implications of dietary reform in the life and works of the authority under consideration. Williams could not assume that his readers had extensive knowledge of the dietary views of Seneca or Dr. Cheyne or Shelley, to name only three of the fifty included, and he therefore printed long extracts from the works of the authorities. In a review of the 1896 edition of the book, Salt argued that it was a storehouse of learning on humane dietetics and man's relations with animals. He also praised it for giving converts courage to continue with their dietary experiments. *Ethics of Diet* made a profound impression on Salt, just as Salt's own book on vegetarianism was to influence Gandhi.

THE BEGINNING OF THE END

The beginning of the end of Salt as a Respectable undoubtedly occurred with J. L. Joynes's leaving Eton. Joynes, impressed with *Progress and Poverty,* traveled with Henry

George to Ireland in the summer of 1882. George had argued, in *The Irish Land Question,* for the nationalization of land in Ireland, and his plan to restore land to the people brought him to the attention of both revolutionary and conventional groups.[25] Salt's account of the Irish trip is brief and accurate: "By a ridiculous blunder of the Irish Constabulary, the two were arrested and locked up as dangerous conspirators; and, though they were quickly discharged when the magistrates discovered the error, the whole Press of the country rang with amused comments. The Government had to apologize to Henry George as an American citizen; and an account of the fiasco, written by Joynes, and published in *The Times,* caused great scandal in Etonian circles . . . ." *The Times,* after publishing Joynes's first dispatch—"A Political Tour of Ireland"—on September 4, 1882, refused to print the later installments. Editorial comments in Conservative newspapers denounced Joynes as "a pretentious prig" and a "shallow globe-trotter." Joynes's standing at Eton was further damaged when Kegan Paul, Trench & Co., George's English publisher, announced the forthcoming publication in its entirety of Joynes's *The Adventures of a Tourist in Ireland.* The headmaster immediately informed young Joynes that he must choose between his mastership and his book. Joynes chose his book and resigned. The pamphlet which brought about his downfall was a deft and pointed exposé of the Irish landlords' cruel treatment of peasants. Lucidly written, impressionistic but factual, *The Adventures of a Tourist in Ireland* is in many respects a model for much of the socially conscious propaganda which was to follow from the pens of Joynes and Salt.[26]

After his "disgrace," Joynes became associated with the

Democratic Federation, which became the Social Democratic Federation in 1884. The Salts were introduced to his new friends—Henry Mayers Hyndman, leader of the Social Democratic Federation, Edward Carpenter, Henry George, William Morris, John Burns, and Belfort Bax. Both Salt and Joynes were in the forefront of the clever young men who threw in with the socialist cause.

Salt's advanced social views were to bring him notoriety at Eton, but his conversion to vegetarianism was causing even greater scandal. Convinced that animals should not be slaughtered, that he could no longer be a "cannibal," Salt had chosen what he considered a saner diet. His colleagues thought his life was in jeopardy; they were also unable to understand the ethical principle he was espousing—"Don't you think that animals were *sent* us as food?" one scientist asked him. Salt stayed on at Eton for two years after the departure of Jim Joynes, but the conviction grew on him that Eton masters "were but cannibals in cap and gown—almost literally cannibals, as devouring the flesh and blood of . . . animals . . . , and indirectly cannibals, as living by the sweat and toil of the classes who do the hard work of the world."[27]

A NEW LIFE

The conversion of Henry S. Salt was complete. Only the leave-taking remained. Salt's account of his final interview with Dr. Edmond Warre, headmaster of Eton, quoted in the introduction, is the perfect illustration of the conventional attitudes which the Salts wished to escape. Salt recalled, in *Seventy Years Among Savages,* Warre's incomprehension of the intellectual and ethical changes which had occurred in Salt; the headmaster was reduced to crying out, "Socialism! Then blow us up, blow us up."

Shaw says, though his figures are not entirely accurate, that Salt was trying to save enough money to buy a pension of £800 a year, but when he read Capenter on "the simple life," he learned "it could be lived on £160 a year," exactly the amount Salt had accumulated, so he left Eton immediately.[28] What Carpenter said in his essay on "Simplification of Life" was that £100 a year would be enough for a family to live on reasonably.[29] Salt says he read Carpenter's essays while at Eton and learned that "it was possible to dispense with the greater part of the trappings with which we are encumbered, and to live far more simply and cheaply than was dreamed of in polite society."[30] Salt's statement has a Thoreauvian ring to it, and he had apparently read about Thoreau and simplification of life in Carpenter's essays. Carpenter the reformer and social critic appealed greatly to him, for Carpenter reconfirmed his own growing dissatisfaction with society and its institutions. Salt did realize that he had come from the privileged classes and that it was by choice that he could put aside money, servants, and an established place in the social order when he adopted the "simple life."

There was still one thing left to do before Salt turned completely to his new life—he needed to criticize the system of education at Eton. He chose to write a scholarly essay in *The Nineteenth Century* pointing out the disadvantages of the tutorial system and the inertia which kept meaningful reform from being made in the system, and proposing a reduction of emphasis on classical work and the introduction of modern subjects. Such a move was unpopular because the classical masters were prosperous and did not want change.

Salt also thought schoolwork should be done under closer supervision, with choice of time and method of preparation not left to the boys' discretion. He wanted to eliminate many traditional holidays and lengthen the time spent concentrating on studies.[31] He called for reducing the size of divisions, but classical tutors, who received large fees for tutorials, were opposed to such a change. Salt argued that despite opposition from reluctant masters, a reform-minded headmaster could easily make significant changes at the college. He was much more optimistic about the prospects for reform than he was to be in a few years, after he had seen how difficult it was to change people and institutions. The article itself caused a great stir; Warre wrote of it in his diary: "Spiteful in tone? A little indecent in haste?"[32] However, Salt's former tutor, F. W. Cornish, told Salt that the longer he contemplated Salt's views, the more convinced he was of their accuracy.[33]

The Salts left Eton at the end of 1884. When the Eton article appeared, they had already begun their simple life in a cottage near Tilford.

NOTES

1. Bernard Shaw, preface to Stephen Winsten's *Salt and His Circle* (London: Hutchinson, 1951), p. 10.

2. I am indebted to Catherine Mandeville Salt and to Denis Salt for making a typescript of E. M. Salt's diary available to me.

3. Henry S. Salt, *Company I Have Kept* (London: George Allen & Unwin, 1930), p. 18.

4. Henry S. Salt, *Cum Grano: Verses and Epigrams* (Berkeley Heights, N.J.: Oriole Press, 1931), p. 142.

5. Moultrie was the grandson of John Moultrie of Charleston, S.C., who was lieutenant governor of East Florida and maintained his allegiance to the Crown during the Revolution. See *Dictionary of National Biography,* XXXIX, 202–4.

6. Salt's most complete account of his relatives is in *Company I Have Kept.*

7. Henry S. Salt, *Seventy Years Among Savages* (London: George Allen & Unwin, 1921), p. 18.

8. *Ibid.,* pp. 16–17.

9. Henry S. Salt, *Memories of Bygone Eton* (London: Hutchinson, 1928), p. 28.

10. Salt, *Company I Have Kept,* p. 25.

11. C. Kegan Paul, *Memories* (London: Kegan Paul, Trench, Truebner, 1899), p. 207.

12. Salt, *Memories of Bygone Eton,* p. 254.

13. O.E. [Henry S. Salt], *Eton under Hornby* (London: A. C. Fifield, 1910), pp. 125–26.

14. Salt, *Seventy Years Among Savages,* p. 36.

15. *Ibid.,* p. 47.

16. *Ibid.,* pp. 52–53.

17. Edward Carpenter, *My Days and Dreams* (New York: Charles Scribner's Sons, 1916), p. 237.

18. Kate Salt to Edward Carpenter, Dec. 27, 1901, Carpenter Collection, Sheffield Public Library, Sheffield, England. All letters from the Carpenter Collection cited in this book are published with permission.

19. Shaw, preface to Winsten, *Salt and His Circle,* p. 9.

20. See Frank Harris, *Bernard Shaw* (London: Victor Gollancz, 1931), pp. 234–38; Stephen Winsten, *Jesting Apostle* (London: Hutchinson, 1956), pp. 115–16; St. John Irvine, *Bernard Shaw* (New York: William Morrow, 1956), pp. 315–16. Janet Dunbar in *Mrs. G.B.S.* (New York: Harper and Row, 1963), casts doubt on the claim that the Shaw marriage was not consummated, pp. 153–54.

21. Salt, *Seventy Years Among Savages,* p. 62.

22. Henry Salt, "The Joy That Never Palls," *Progress,* VI (Nov., 1886), 456.

23. Catherine Mandeville Salt to Bernard Shaw, May 30, 1939; copy in the British Library.

24. Salt, *Seventy Years Among Savages,* pp. 62–63; *Vegetarian Review,* Oct., 1896, pp. 467–69.

25. For an excellent discussion, see Elwood P. Lawrence, *Henry George in the British Isles* (East Lansing: Michigan State University Press, 1957), pp. 13–29.

26. Salt, *Seventy Years Among Savages*, p. 58; J. L. Joynes, *The Adventures of a Tourist in Ireland* (London: Kegan Paul, Trench, 1882), p. iv; Lawrence, *Henry George in the British Isles*, pp. 21–22.

27. Salt, *Seventy Years Among Savages*, p. 64.

28. Shaw, preface to Winsten, *Salt and His Circle*, p. 9. GBS's memory was failing when he wrote the preface. He confused Eton and Cambridge, Melville and Merivale, and was often inaccurate on specific details.

29. Edward Carpenter, *England's Ideal* (London: Swan Sonnenschein, Lowrey, 1887), p. 98.

30. Salt, *Seventy Years Among Savages*, p. 73.

31. H. S. Salt, "Confessions of an Eton Master," *The Nineteenth Century*, XVII (Jan., 1885), 170–84.

32. Salt, *Memories of Bygone Eton*, p. 229.

33. *Ibid.*

CHAPTER

2

Henry Salt: Socialist and Follower of the Simple Life

"In the 'eighties there were two movements especially attractive to one who was breaking away from the old academical traditions, to wit, Socialism, the more equitable distribution of wealth; and Simplification, the saner method of living."

Seventy Years Among Savages

The Salts did not just take up a new residence in 1885; rather they began a new life, what Salt was to call "an emigration, a romance, a strange new life in some remote antipodes, where the emblems of the old servitude, such as cap and gown, found new and better uses. . . ."[1] Salt's top hat came to provide shade for a young vegetable marrow (squash), and his gown was cut into strips to fasten vines to a wall. At the cottage near Tilford, the Salts lived without servants, entertained their new friends, and worked for socialist causes. Two of their new acquaintances were Thoreauvians who obviously enforced the Salts' own views on Simplification. The first was Edward Carpenter, the titular deity of the Salt household, and the second was W. J. Jupp, a Congregational minister who had left the church to found an ethical religious group.

Edward Carpenter was a Whitmanian as well as a Thoreauvian, and his *Towards Democracy,* written under the direct influence of Whitman, was much read and admired in revolutionary circles; its homo-erotic overtones made it a special favorite of those who were in doubt about their sexual identities or who had found their role as homosexuals. Carpenter's Thoreau-inspired life on a farm, his glorification of manual labor and the simple life were important influences on the Salts. His long correspondence with the Salts demonstrates their easy friendship and common interests. Salt was explicit about his indebtedness to Carpenter when he wrote Dr. S. A. Jones in 1890, ". . . it was through him that I first became acquainted with *Walden*, and furthermore was induced to give up my educational work at Eton College . . . and adopt a simpler and more independent style of life."[2]

Salt characterized the other Thoreauvian, W. J. Jupp, as a nature lover who "brought us tidings of the greatest of poet naturalists, Henry David Thoreau. . . ."[3] Since Salt had already read about Thoreau in Carpenter's essays, it is most likely that Salt is referring to Jupp's emphasis on Thoreau as naturalist. In Jupp's gentle autobiography, *Wayfarings: A Record of Adventure and Liberation in the Life of the Spirit,* there is a long chapter devoted to Thoreau. Jupp presented Thoreau not only as naturalist and individualist but also as a "relentless thinker and searcher for truth."[4] Thoreau was intent, Jupp believed, on facing reality, on escaping the shams and shibboleths of civilization. The essay is convincing and full of ethical interpretations of the Concordian, and it is obvious that Jupp's views on Thoreau had considerable influence on Salt.

SALT AND HIS REFORMER FRIENDS

The cottage at Tilford was a way station between academia and the world of reform. It was this simple life at Tilford which offered Shaw material for one of his most engaging comic essays, "A Sunday on the Surrey Hills." GBS cast himself in the role of a cockney who hated the country but allowed himself to be enticed by his friends the Salts to spend a weekend there. According to GBS, Salt, though "a man of exceptional intelligence on most subjects, is country mad, and keeps a house at a hole called Tilford, down Farnham way, to which he retires at intervals, subsisting on the fungi of the neighborhood, and writing articles advocating that line of diet and justifying the weather and the season to 'pent-up' London. He entertained no doubt that a day at Tilford would convert me from rurophobia to rurolatry; and as he is a sensible companion for a walk and a talk—if only he would, like a sensible man, confine himself to the Thames Embankment—I at last consented to the experiment. . . ."[5]

A whole series of calamities awaited GBS—he had a long walk in the rain to the Salt cottage, his clothes shrunk after they were put by the fire to dry, he caught a cold and was subjected to Mrs. Salt's home remedies. There were misadventures on his walks with Salt in the rain and mud: he gave a cow a friendly slap and water squirted up to his armpit. Mrs. Salt talked at length about the gentleness of her dog, but her husband had to frustrate the dog's attempts to chase the water-drenched sheep.

Salt, in *Seventy Years Among Savages,* praised GBS as one perfectly attuned to life in a house without domestic help.

Shaw was, he said, "conscientious and exemplary" in washing up, and made his bed with "methodical precision." The local Farnham paper, however, did not recall GBS's visit with fondness or praise; years later, Salt reported, the paper scathingly denounced the *Pall Mall Gazette* article and its author, referring to him as "a cockney gentleman possessing a very fine liver, but no soul above his stomach."[6]

Salt's major contacts with the reformers were, at first, as they had been at Eton, through his brother-in-law, Jim Joynes. After being forced to leave Eton, young Joynes had joined several groups, including the Social Democratic Federation (as it was finally to be called), the Fellowship of the New Life, and the Fabians. The socialist groups were fragmented—often warring among themselves,[7] for there were Marxian and non-Marxian, Christian and rationalist groups. Joynes was able to work with many opposing organizations; for example, he knew and worked with both Hyndman and William Morris. Salt was welcomed into these circles, and he met such reformers and revolutionaries as Sidney Olivier, William Morris, Graham Wallas, the Webbs, Hyndman, Bax, and Prince Kropotkin. Unfortunately, there is little correspondence of Salt with these reformers, for he saw them frequently in the country or in London, and seldom needed to write them.

EARLY CONTRIBUTIONS TO RADICAL JOURNALS

A major outlet for Salt's social criticism was *Justice,* the Social Democratic Federation journal which was founded in 1884 with funds provided by Carpenter. Jim Joynes was a prolific contributor to the journal, and Salt obviously had easy access to *Justice*'s pages. Several of his essays and poems of this period will be quoted in whole or in part in this chapter; they are forcefully written and indicate the spirit and tone of his early reform writings better than any paraphrase could do. Salt's first contribution to *Justice,* written before he left Eton and published on October 25, 1884 (p. 2), was a sardonic poem:

CHARITY ON THE CHEAP

. . . the Commissioners of her Majesty's Works and Public Buildings intend to distribute this autumn among the working classes and the poor inhabitants of London, the surplus bedding-out plants in Battersea, Hyde, the Regent's and Victoria Parks. . . . *Daily News, Oct. 13th.*

Methinks that few could read without a smile,—
    Though, sure, there is small reason for hilarity—
This latest effort in the pot-herb style
      Of Christian Charity.

'Tis Christian Charity in Christian land,—
    Forgive the blasphemy, ye heavenly Powers!—
That offers to a foodless, homeless band
      Her—"surplus flowers."

See yonder wretch, upon whose haggard brow
    In plain deep-furrowed lines is writ Starvation:
He cries for bread; and will ye give him now
      A rich—carnation?

See yonder woman, fallen, starved, debased;
    In piteous mute appeal her hand she raises;
And Christian Charity brings forth in haste
      A pot of—daisies.

Yon children, too, that in the gutters sport
    With famine-stricken eyes and pallid blue lips;
What gift has Charity for these? Why, nought:—
      Except some tulips.

'Fore God, I do respect the pagan code
 Of undisguised neglect and sheer barbarity,
Above this sentimental, flowery mode
 Of Christian Charity.

Salt continued his mocking attack upon the English *laissez-faire* economic system in his first contribution to *Justice* after he left the confines of Eton. On February 14, 1885 (p. 5), he published a poem in which he consciously identified himself with the British working man:

A SONG OF "FREEDOM"

I marvel that no poet sings
 Of "individual Freedom,"
And what unnumbered gifts she brings—
 Except to those who need 'em.

Her choicest favours fall, we see,
 On this enfranchised nation;
Free contract, competition free,
 Free trade, and free—starvation.

   . . . .

We British workmen, so they say,
 Are free; and who can doubt it?
For if we do not like our pay,
 We're free—to go without it.

   . . . .

Thus free-men all our lives are we,
 Each in his own vocation;
And when old age is come, we're free—
 To die of slow starvation.

So, hey! for England's glorious rights;
 Free sellin' and free buyin';

> Free libraries; free pews; free fights;
> And a free ditch—to die in!

Salt's identification with the working classes does have its romantic aspects, for whatever his intellectual sympathies were (and they were considerable), his speech and manners were those of a university man. He was not then, nor was he to be, a workingman; but *Justice* was a newspaper devoted to propaganda, and perhaps one should not object to Salt's identification with the workingman in his poem. In other of his amusing, satiric poems he was more detached, more restrained, and more effective.

H. M. Hyndman, in his unreliable but evocative autobiography, *The Record of an Adventurous Life,* recalled that the circulation of *Justice* was small and that many of the staff took to Fleet Street and the Strand to sell copies. It was, he said, a "curious scene": William Morris in blue suit and soft hat; Champion, Frost, and Joynes in "the morning garments of the well-to-do"; working-class comrades; and Hyndman in frock coat.[8] Salt was not mentioned as a participant in the peddling of *Justice* in the heart of London; but the romantic spirit he adopted in his early socialist phase was quite similar to that described by Hyndman.

In Salt's first essays for *Justice,* his superior literary skills, produced by the best educational insitutions in England, are particularly noticeable. His first essay, "Schoolboy Charity," was published on January 17, 1885 (p. 4), soon after he left Eton. It is reprinted here in its entirety.

One of the most remarkable signs of the inability of the upper classes to understand the true significance of the social question is to be seen in the "Missions" which are being established by several public schools in the poorest quarters of London and other cities.

The authorities of these schools have apparently come to the praiseworthy conclusion that they ought to interest the minds of their pupils as much as possible in the lower classes, and the result has been the establishment of these "Missions," of which the largest and most important is the "Eton Mission" in Hackney Wick. The object of these institutions is of course primarily the moral improvement of the schoolboys, by whose subscriptions they are supported, efforts being made to keep the boys acquainted with the condition of the district in which the "Mission" is situated, and occasionally to induce some of them to visit the place and take a personal interest in the people. A secondary object, indirectly aimed at, is the benefit of the poor people themselves.

Now, as regards the first of these objects, we may at once admit that the question whether the sons of aristocrats and plutocrats who support these "Missions" are likely to derive much moral good from it themselves, is not one in which we are greatly interested. But we may remark, in passing, that it is hardly possible that boys who merely subscribe, or rather get their parents to subscribe for them, a small sum which will in no way affect their personal comfort, can be greatly influenced by the action. Boys are naturally thoughtless, and will never be much moved by the accounts of suffering, however harrowing, which they only hear of through sermons and lectures. Personal visits are, of course, impossible, except in a very few cases; with the mass of the school the collection must soon sink into an ordinary periodical subscription, and the whole subject is voted a "bore."

On the other hand, as regards the people of the district in which any such "Mission" is planted, it cannot be too often or too strongly stated that these charitable institutions, though they may alleviate the sufferings of individuals, tend inevitably to postpone the general and final emancipation of the poor. It seems at first sight ungracious to criticise and condemn what is doubtless a well-intentioned scheme; but it must in candour be said that far more harm than good is likely to result from such injudicious attempts to bridge over the gulf between class and class, without in the least understanding the nature or the cause of this gulf. The real healing of the wound is rendered more and more difficult by these half-remedies and quack-medicines, which only leave the sufferer in the same helpless condition in which they found him. The true issue is obscured by this mistaken doctrine of "Charity," which makes those who give imagine that they have done their duty towards solving the great social problem, and inspires those who receive with a false sense of an obligation that does not exist. For if the authorities of English public schools are really desirous of enlightening their pupils on the subject of social inequality, why do they not invite them to consider what is the source from which their parents' money is derived? Why not propose as a subject for a school essay the meaning of "having £5000 a year"? Why not bid the boys consider how it is that they and their parents are fed, clothed, and supported in life-long luxury, without being compelled to do a single stroke of work? That would be a far more instructive manner of arousing their pupils' sympathy with the lower classes than the present method of asking them to subscribe ten shillings each, and then feel the proud consciousness of having done a charitable act. As has often been pointed out, Justice, and not Charity, is the one power that can satisfactorily deal with this great social question, but unfortunately our rich folk are far more inclined to the consideration of charity than of Justice. The mischief of all such institutions as the "Eton Mission" is that they salve the conscience of the rich subscriber, and make him far less likely to give the question his full and earnest consideration; while on the other hand they stave off the just discontent of the poor and prevent their seeing the enormity of the robbery which is daily perpetrated on them.

If a number of school-boys, after plundering a poor man's orchard and regaling themselves to repletion on his fruit, were to send him a rosy apple out of commiseration of his poverty and by way of moral discipline to themselves, we should probably remark that they are adding insult to injury. Yet it would be a tolerably correct illustration of what is now being done by the "Eton Mission" and similar public-school charity.

This obviously socialist analysis has a decided Thoreauvian ring. Salt was able to point out almost mockingly the ineffectiveness of the project upon the schoolboys themselves. While he could have been much more savage in his denuciation, even in the first flush of his conversion to socialism, he is restrained. It is clear that the author is not a workingman, nor does he claim a birthright which is not his; rather, the tone is that a well-educated observer lashing out, with the language at his disposal, against the injustices of late-Victorian society.

Similarly, in an essay entitled "Thou Shalt Not Steal," published in *Justice* on March 14, 1885 (p. 2), Salt noted:

"stealing" cannot in justice be limited to the narrow conventional sense in which it is at present used. If to steal is to take what is rightfully the property of another, there is many a rich man whose possessions are fully secured by law, who is as much a thief as many a Dartmoor convict. Nay more, there may be such a thing as an unintentional and unpremeditated stealing; indeed the whole system of modern society, with its "profits" and "interests," and similar genteel phrases, is nothing else than a gigantic contravention of the eighth commandment, by which non-workers steal the produce of the labouring classes. The fact that individuals cannot remedy this systematic wrong does not in the least disprove the existence of the evil; at any rate they ought to have the grace to acknowledge the source from which their comforts are derived, and to join in the attempt to bring about as speedy a reform as possible. Unfortunately this is a course to which the capitalist classes seems

specially disinclined. They insist that they are the rightful pos-
sessors of wealth which comes in to them without any labour on
their part, and attempt to raise the cry of "Stop thief" against those
who venture even to investigate the origin of their wealth. Our
capitalists persist to the bitter end in the fatuous assertion that to
live idly on the labour of others is not the same thing as to steal.

One of Salt's most effective articles was a short essay in
Justice on July 11, 1885 (p. 5), entitled "Fashionable
Cricket," which concerned the annual Eton-Harrow cricket
match and contained Salt's strongly worded and provocative
speculations on what the poor might do if they recognized
that their toil made all the display of wealth possible. That
Salt saw redress coming more quickly than it did is also
obvious to the modern reader.

To-day all fashionable London is assembled at Lord's Cricket
Ground to witness the annual match between Eton and Harrow. It
is the great gala day of the West End, a day of festivities and
sumptuous luncheons, and champagne-cup and general deification
of the youthful heroes of our two great aristocratic and plutocratic
schools. To-day every fashionable person will undoubtedly wear a
light-blue or a dark-blue rosette. It is really astonishing how much
artificial excitement can be got up about a colour. We read that
during the latter centuries of the Roman Empire the several
factions of the Circus, the Whites, the Reds, the Blues, the
Greens, became the one absorbing topic of interest in many of the
chief cities; and this rivalry grew to such a pitch, that riots and
bloodshed were often the consequence. Equally childish, though
happily less serious in its results, is the flutter of excitement caused
by the Eton and Harrow cricket-match, the contest between the
Light Blues and the Dark. It is natural enough that the school-boys
themselves and their immediate friends and relations, should be
inclined to regard these contests as very important events; for a rage

for athleticism is now-a-days the chief feature of public school education; but it is really surprising that some ten or twelve thousand persons, besides those directly interested in the two schools, should range themselves as partisans on one side or the other. Can it be that the denizens of the West End find time hangs rather heavy on their hands?
. . . .

Meanwhile another struggle is going on, none the less real because it is not fashionable cricket and not reported in West End newspapers. This is no three days contest, but one which has been waged for at least three centuries. But now it is said that a return match will shortly be played in which the Rich will find themselves disposed of for a pretty score in a very summary fashion, being caught, stumped, clean-bowled, and run out, in a manner which will be entirely gratifying to everyone who has the least sympathy with the cause of Justice and Right, though undoubtedly somewhat distasteful to those who have long held a selfish monopoly of wealth and enjoyment.

Had not Salt left his active work in socialist propaganda, he might well have been a major figure in the movement toward social reform, for there is in his writing a clarity of expression and an air of passionate indignation at the excesses of capitalism. Certainly a reader is more drawn to Salt's essays than to the turgid prose of Sidney and Beatrice Webb. Jim Joynes also had a lively prose style, and these two, along with Shaw, were among the most effective writers in the various socialist organizations.

FREE THOUGHT AND VEGETARIANISM

Salt's wit and stinging social satire permeates his essay "Fasting and Feasting," which appeared in *Justice* on April 4,

1885 (p. 4). Salt's personal preferences for free thought and vegetarianism undoubtedly made him more severe in his criticism of the religious fasting in the West End during Lent. He was scornful of those who mortified the flesh during Lent, for, he maintained, practical people who thought for themselves found it "difficult to understand how a system of occasional semi-starvation can be either pleasing to God, or beneficial to man." He did concede that eating too little, for religious reasons, was better than eating too much. He found fasting in the West End to be hyprocritical, since the wealthy citizens of that area inaugurated Lent with a meal of tasty salt fish and continued to eat fish on Fridays. Good Friday itself, he noted, was not completely a day of abstinence, since hot cross buns were allowed. He concluded his section on fasting in fashionable London by noting that the wealthy had devised delightful ways to exercise their piety and to gain favor with God.

As contrast, Salt wrote that

the inhabitants of the opposite quarter of London will be found at the end of this week to have fasted more strictly, though of course less "on principle" than their neighbours of the West. Eminent physicians have affirmed that the poor people of the East End suffer mainly from one disease, and that is *starvation*. To these the Lenten fast is a fast indeed; only it must be noted that it does not differ in this respect from any other period of the year; it is not preceded and followed by a feast. Ash Wednesday is here too a day of sackcloth and ashes, with the slight difference that there is no mention of salt-fish, that part of the ritual being confined to more fashionable quarters. Good Friday brings with it as severe an abstinence as the Church could require; so much so, that hot-cross buns are of the very rarest occurrence, and the day is not generally felt to deserve

37

(in the East End at any rate) the appellation of "Good." "Holy Week" it can scarcely be called; yet after all it is not more unholy than any other, in a region where starvation reigns equally all the year round. And lastly Easter brings with it, in the East End, no resurrection of hope, for the hopes of these poor people have long been buried—to rise no more. The West End may break the monotony of its feasting by occasionally playing at a fast; but in the East End it is a perpetual and unbroken Lent.

Let those amateur ascetics who sit down to an abundant table on Easter Sunday bethink them of this fact, which concerns them more closely than they may imagine. Every *plus* has its corresponding *minus,* and every feast has its corresponding fast. The luxury of the West End is the true, the inevitable cause of the destitution of the East, and until the former is removed it is worse than useless to prate about remedying the latter. To search out the cause of the great social blot, this cancer that eats away the heart of our brutal civilization; to face the question boldly, with the determination that, come what may, justice shall be done, even to the detriment of "private interests"; to resolve that an end shall be put to the iniquitous system under which one half of the population of London is for ever fasting that the other half may feast; this would be a more truly religious act, more acceptable to God because more serviceable to man, than to go through the mockery of pretending to fast during forty days of the year, while over-eating oneself largely during the remaining three hundred and twenty-five.

This essay is a particularly good example of Salt's indebtedness to Thoreau and Shelley, for both of these writers were interested in food reform as well as social reform.

OTHER REFORMERS

In a brief essay on William Cobbett, Salt points out to reformers interested in the single-tax theories of Henry

George an earlier publication of a native Englishman who anticipated many of George's ideas. The emotional response of English socialists to George was a strong one: Shaw declared that five-sixths of those in the Socialist Revival of 1883 "had been converted by Henry George," and it was from hearing George speak that Shaw began his own conversion to socialism.[9] Salt was beginning to assume the role of scholar, and in his essay on Cobbett in the June 6, 1885, issue of *Justice* (p. 2), he drew to readers' attention Cobbett's contribution to the literature of Land Reform. His opening paragraph gives the flavor of his argument:

It is just fifty years since William Cobbett published his "Legacy to Labourers," so-called, as he himself tells us, because he wished the book, after his death, to be "an inmate of the cottages of England." The main object of the book was to prove by historical references that landlords have no absolute right to the land, but merely hold it under the monarch, who is the representative of the people. Landlords have the *use* of the land, but it is not, strictly speaking, their *own;* nor have they the right to drive the natives from the land, so as to cause them to perish of hunger or cold. The "Legacy to Labourers" is full throughout of interest to Land Reformers, for many of Henry George's strongest points will be found to be there anticipated; but perhaps the two subjects which Cobbett treats of with most vigor and success are the "burning questions"—as burning now as then—of the administration of the Poor Laws and compulsory emigration. The iniquitous Poor Law of 1834 was then attracting the notice of the country, and Cobbett denounces with fierce invective and righteous scorn the new system of "making it so irksome and painful to obtain any relief, as to prevent people from applying for it." The economists and philanthropists of the day were recommending the practice of appointing strangers to be the keepers of work houses—"firm men, not to be moved by distress, whether feigned or real." "Are we in *Eng-*

land," asks Cobbett, "or are we in *hell,* while we are reading this?" He points out that the inevitable effect of a system like this would be that "nobody, except poor, wretched, feeble-minded as well as feeble-bodied souls, would ever apply for relief. There being no parish relief, the labourers would be compelled to receive whatever wages the farmers chose to give them. For life is precious to every living creature. After exhausting all the resources of supplication, after wives and children had pleaded in vain with streaming eyes the labouring man must submit." Let the present condition of the working classes testify how amply the events of the last fifty years have fulfilled this prophecy of Cobbett's! Yet the very class which passed the Poor Law of 1834 now appoints a Royal Commission to enquire into the Housing of the Poor, and affects to be surprised at finding them in a condition which has been directly brought about by its own greed and selfishness!

SALT AND LITERARY CRITICISM

The preceding examples give a fair sampling of Salt's nonliterary contributions to *Justice* during his active participation in the affairs of that journal. Salt also distinguished himself as a literary critic, for *Justice* and for other socialist journals, during the first years after he left Eton. His contributions added prestige to the standing of these journals among the intellectual socialists who subscribed to them. Salt undertook serious criticism of a wide range of English and American authors: Thoreau, Melville, Hawthorne, Poe, Tennyson, Shelley, James Thomson (B. V.), De Quincey, and others. In the first of these critical essays, on Thoreau, published in *Justice* on November 14, 1885 (p. 2), Salt was more propagandistic than in his later literary writings, for he worked overly hard to bring Thoreau near to the socialist camp:

Among those American writers who have denounced the anomalies and tyranny of Transatlantic government and society none have done so more eloquently than Henry Thoreau. Though not a professed Socialist, but appealing rather to the individual capabilities of man, Thoreau deserves to be attentively studied by every social reformer; his chief book, "Walden," being not only remarkable for its intensity of moral purpose and high literary power, but containing also the record of a very interesting experiment in practical life. . . .

In "Walden" we find the essence of Thoreau's teaching, and also the record of his experiences of unconventional life. He found that by working about six weeks in the year he could meet all the expenses of living, and have free for study the whole of his winters as well as most of his summers—a discovery which might throw considerable light on the solution of certain social problems in our own country. Even if we allow an ample margin for the peculiar circumstances of his case, and the favourable conditions under which he made his experiment, the conclusion seems to be inevitable that the burden of labour which falls on the human race is not only very unfairly distributed but is also unnecessarily heavy. Thoreau did a real service to the cause of Socialism by practically demonstrating the truth of Socialist calculations and proving how little labour is sufficient to support mankind. We may regret that he did not proceed to the question "What then becomes of all the immeasurable wealth produced by the vast labour of our toilers in town and country who are themselves left in a condition of life-long penury and want?" On this social question Thoreau does not enter; but confines himself to showing what every individual may do in the way of simplicity and self-help. He cannot claim therefore to give any complete solution of the great social problem; for it is obvious that no amount of self-help can by itself avail much in the overwhelming struggle for existence that is going on in every great town. An inhabitant of Concord might walk out a mile or two and build himself a hut by Walden Pond; but there is no such refuge to the dweller in the East End of London; Victoria Park does not offer the advantages of Walden. Still there is no doubt that Thoreau's teaching is perfectly true as far as it goes; the world is not yet sufficiently awake to the fact that a great part of its evils are due to luxury, extravagance, and a foolish striving after unnecessary "comforts" and personal possessions. On many points Thoreau's opinions will commend themselves to all Socialists. He insists on the advisability of some education, in manual work instead of the usual flimsy university education. He condemns the factory system where the condition of the workmen is daily becoming worse and worse[,] "Not that mankind may be well and honestly clad but that Corporations may be enriched." He has discovered that "trade curses everything it handles," and that the "model farms," of modern days are huge delusions and impostures. "A model farm! Stocked with men! A great grease spot, redolent of manures and buttermilk! Under a high state of cultivation, being manured with the hearts and brains of men! As if you were to raise your potatoes in the churchyard! Such is the model farm." Very severe too are his strictures on the profit-mongering, manslaughtering Railway systems of America. "We do not ride on the railroad, it rides upon us. Did you ever think what those 'sleepers' are that underlie the railroad? Each one is a man, an Irishman or a Yankee man. They are sound sleepers, I can assure you. And every few years a new lot is laid down and run over; so that if some have the pleasure of riding on a rail others have the misfortune to be ridden upon." But in no part of "Walden" is the writing more vigorous and trenchant than when Thoreau is expressing his contempt for the cant and humbug of "charity" and "philanthropy." Doing-good, he says, is one of the professions that are full and if he knew that a man was coming to his house to do him good he should run for his life. So too with charity. "It may be that he who bestows the largest amount of time and money on the needy is doing the utmost by his mode of life to produce that misery which he strives in vain to relieve. It is the pious slave-breeder devoting the proceeds of every tenth slave to buy a Sunday's liberty for the rest."

I will conclude with a quotation from "Walden" which might easily be mistaken for one of the most eloquent passages in Henry George's "Progress and Poverty." It is on the subject of modern civilisation. "But how do the poor minority fare? Perhaps it will be found that just in proportion as some have been placed in outward circumstances above the savage, others have been degraded below him. The luxury of one class is counterbalanced by the indigence of another. On the one side is the palace, on the other are the almshouse and 'silent poor.' The myriads who built the Pyramids to be the tombs of the Pharaohs were fed on garlic and it may-be were not decently buried themselves. The mason who finishes the cornice of the palace returns at night perchance to a hut not so good as a wigwam. It is a mistake to suppose that in a country where the usual evidences of civilization exist, the condition of a very large body of the inhabitants may not be as degraded as that of savages. Such to a greater or less extent, is the condition of the operatives of every denomination in England, which is the great workhouse of the world."

Though he makes too great an effort to bring Thoreau into the socialist camp, Salt is not intellectually dishonest in his presentation, for he admits that Thoreau was not a professing socialist but a master of self-reliance and individualism. The quotations are well taken, especially the one on philanthropy. It is well-written, sympathetic, brief article, one of the first to appear in England after R. L. Stevenson's savage attack on Thoreau in the *Cornhill Magazine* in 1880. Interesting as it may be in itself, it gives us clues, as we shall see in later sections, to Salt's development, for within five years he was to produce his excellent study on Thoreau.

Another of Salt's literary favorites was Shelley, and he developed views on Shelley not held in respectable circles, as his *Justice* essay, published October 31, 1885 (p. 2), and entitled "Shelley's Views on Social Reform," demonstrates.

Salt viewed Shelley as the greatest of England's lyric poets, but the poet had an even greater claim to fame, since he was an aristocrat brought up in an atmosphere of luxury, and yet he "devoted the whole power of his genius to the cause of the people, and impressed all who knew him with the conviction that he was the noblest and most unselfish of men. Alike in social questions, politics, and religion, he was an ardent and uncompromising champion of the people's rights and true liberty of thought and action; and his whole life testified to the perfect sincerity of his opinions, for he suffered much from calumny and persecution."

Salt regarded Shelley as being the victim of bigots who misrepresented him in their desire to maintain their own social and religious tyranny. Salt argued that it was fallacious to see Shelley as a good poet who had no practical sense. He also attacked what he called the "poor, poor, Shelley" theory which maintained that if the poet "had only had a better education, religious, and moral, together with this, that, and the other advantage, this erring lamb would have developed into one of the most orderly and respectable sheep in all the fold of Orthodoxy. It is needless to state that this ludicrous supposition finds not a trace of evidence to support it in the study of Shelley's life, writings, or character, and is only adopted by those who have never really grasped or appreciated the value of his opinions."

Salt noted that in the notes to "Queen Mab" Shelley exposed the curses which resulted from luxury and wealth.

Salt maintained that Shelley knew that occupations such as farming were essential but were held in contempt by society and that those employed in useless arts, such as jewelers and actors, gained fame and wealth. Shelley also traced the moral degradations of cities to wealth, and saw the remedy for the wrongs of society as the overthrow of the capitalist system.

Salt concluded his essay on Shelley with the statement he was to reiterate in many of his later studies: Shelley employed "the loftiest political inspiration as a means towards hastening the emancipation of the people and the overthrow of every kind of social tyranny and injustice."

Salt's essays on literary figures were not confined to authors he found personally pleasing or rewarding. He also wrote on Lord Tennyson, a poet whose philosophy (at least in later years) was conservative and bellicose. Salt's views were encapsulated in a brief poem, published in *Justice* on May 2, 1885 (p. 5):

TO THE POET LAUREATE.

(On His Reported Self-Sufficiency)

You—you—'tis you have failed to understand
That England's *Workmen* are her all-in-all,
And social wrongs that devastate our land
    Will wreak Old England's fall
    Be navies small or great.

In twaddling rhymes that move the reader's mirth
You bid us lord it over land and sea—
Poor poet, what are all these pratings worth?
    How sad, to those who struggle to be free,
    Is this thy servile state!

You—you—who once did champion Freedom sweet,
But now prefer a barren title place,—

When workmen starve by thousands, is it meet
  To urge on war apace
  Our Jingo Laureate?

In an earlier issue of *To-day* (February, 1884), Salt published an essay, "The Tennysonian Philosophy," in which, though fully aware of Tennyson's poetic gifts, Salt was scornful of the banality of Tennyson's thought. He harshly noted that Lord Tennyson's philosophical system was a mixture of "opportunism and shallow optimistic theories." Salt was particularly incensed that the doctor in "In the Children's Hospital" brutally informed a nurse that a dying child no longer needed her care. The doctor was a religious disbeliever, and Salt objected to coupling brutality with religious disbelief. He did not deny that such doctors might exist, but he felt it was not belief or disbelief which made them so.[10] Salt continued his analysis by showing that Tennyson constantly argued that happiness in this life depended upon belief in an afterlife. He attacked the Victorian morality attached to the ending of *Idylls of the King,* and he was his most acid in noting that Maud objected to peace and praised the Crimean war. Salt's conclusions on Tennyson are more contemporary than nineteenth century: ". . . while we fully admit the greatness of his purely poetical powers, we have no hesitation in asserting that the *thought* which runs through his writings is as feeble as the *expression* is beautiful. His philosophy, if such it can be called, was false and hollow from the beginning, and has become more and more unscientific with increasing age and intolerance."[11] Nine years later in *Tennyson as a Thinker,* to be discussed in a later section, Salt was even harsher in his indictment of Lord Tennyson and those who praised him.

FELLOWSHIP OF THE NEW LIFE

Salt was testing his ideas in numerous societies and organizations, many of which had also appealed to his brother-in-law, J. L. Joynes, Jr. For example, through Joynes, Salt was brought into the Fellowship of the New Life, which was founded—rather, talked into existence—by the wandering scholar Thomas Davidson. Born in Scotland, he traveled to North America and lived and taught in Boston, Toronto, and St. Louis, and came under the influence of the American Transcendental movement. After an extended stay in Italy, he wandered to London, where in 1883 he gathered together several people with similar ethical views, forming the utopian organization known as the Fellowship of the New Life. According to the minutes of the December 7, 1883, session, the concerns of the Fellowship were:

"Object: The cultivation of a perfect character in each and all.

"Principle: The subordination of material things to spiritual.

"Fellowhip: The sole and essential condition of fellowship shall be a single-minded, sincere, and strenuous devotion to the object and principle."[12]

Jim Joynes was one of sixteen people at the first general meeting, held on October 24, 1883, to hear Davidson. E. R. Pease, in his classic study, *The History of the Fabian Society,* characterized Davidson as "spiritually a descendant of the Utopians of Brook Farm and the Phalanstery, and what he yearned for was something in the nature of a community of superior people withdrawn from the world because of its wickedness. . . ."[13]

According to Pease, after Davidson's presentation that night, the "idea of founding a community abroad was generally discredited, and it was generally recognised that it would not be possible to establish here in England any independent community."[14] Pease seems to have been wrong, for Shaw reported that Salt and Carpenter at one time thought of establishing "land Colonies," though there is no evidence in the Salt-Carpenter correspondence to suppport Shaw's statement. Lord Olivier, however, in a letter to Archibald Henderson, did speak of Davidson's proposed colony in Southern California that would "recreate the World."[15] It is likely that Salt was too much a Thoreauvian to consider such proposals. The Fellowship of the New Life did, however, establish a Fellowship House in London. Edith Lees (who was to marry Havelock Ellis) was a prime mover in this communal group, and she wrote a devastating description of the experiment in her novel *Attainment*. Salt himself does not seem to have been involved in any way in Fellowship House, and he does not mention the project in his autobiographies or in his letters now available. Again, the Thoreauvian view of such plans may well have influenced him. Lees's final view was "Fellowship is Hell."[16]

Though the communal life aspects of the Fellowship did not seemingly appeal to Salt, the ethical approach, based on principles espoused earlier by Emerson and Thoreau, did win his sympathies. J. R. MacDonald, later to be Prime Minister, wrote in *Seed-time,* April, 1892 (p. 1):

When the New Fellowship was started ten years ago, *Progress and Poverty* had just been published. There was then no organised Socialist body in this country, for the Democratic Federation . . .

professed no more revolutionary creed than Land Nationalisation. But the Socialist movement grew rapidly. Within two years there were at least four militant Socialist societies in London. . . . The Socialists were full of fight, and Mr. Hyndman predicted an economic revolution as a centenary commemoration of the political revolution in France. Regimentalism was the order of the day. A moral new order was to follow economic and political change.

The Fellowship, influenced by Thoreau and Emerson rather than by Marx and Hyndman, stood somewhat aloof, although in sympathy with the ideals of the Socialist societies. At the risk of being called diletantist [sic], whilst others were active, it felt that it had to insist upon the necessity of moral reform, as well as of political and economic reform.

Salt contributed articles to *Seed-time,* but he was by this time involved in organizing the Humanitarian League and his time and energy were clearly devoted to this task.

When Shaw wrote the early history of the Fabians in *Fabian Tract No. 41*, he made light of the moral regeneration ideas pervading the Fellowship: "The Fabian Society was warlike in its origin: it came into existence through a schism in an earlier society [the Fellowship of the New Life] for the peaceful regeneration of the race by the cultivation of perfection of individual character. Certain members of that circle, modestly feeling that the revolution would have to wait an unreasonably long time if postponed until they personally had attained perfection, set up the banner of Socialist militant; seceded from the Regenerators; and established themselves independently as the Fabian Society."[17]

Salt joined the Fabians, though his greater sympathies were with the Fellowship. His distress at factionalism (a disturbing problem certainly in socialist groups) was present in much of his thought in the decades which followed, but his views allowed him to embrace many causes, drawing what he considered was best from each. He began to move away from close connections with doctrinaire, activist socialism to the more ethical socialistic views expressed in the following article, "Socialists and Vegetarians," which appeared in *To-day* in November, 1886 (pp. 172–74):

From a recent correspondence in the pages of the *Commonweal,* it appears that there is some danger of our witnessing a very pretty quarrel between Socialists and Vegetarians, in which the former, with the ferocious activity characteristic of the higher carnivora, are disposed to be the aggressors. One would have thought that Socialists had already enough to do in carrying on their crusade against the present system of society; and it certainly is to be regretted that they should devote their superfluous energies to an attack on the votaries of another *ism,* who, if not welcomed as friends, ought, at any rate, not to be regarded as foes. For, in the name of common sense, what antagonism can there rightly be between these two movements? Stupidity and selfishness—these are the true enemies of Socialism, all the world over; and it so happens that they are the enemies of Vegetarianism also, though the fight goes on in other fields, and under other conditions of warfare. It would be a sad pity if any social reformers should waste their power in fighting on the wrong side in this question of diet, and thereby undo with one hand some of the good they have been doing with the other.

"But Vegetarianism," say the Socialists, "is a snare and delusion, because the adoption of food-thrift by the working classes would bring with it a further depression of wages, with the result that the whole advantage would go to the Capitalist." Now, it must be admitted that this objection would be a serious one if Vegetarianism were likely to be suddenly and generally adopted by working men; but when one reflects that the change in diet, if it comes at all, is quite certain to be very gradual, and that Socialists will not be idle in the meantime, the danger of a reduction of wages caused by food-thrift seems to be somewhat imaginary. Let us suppose that in fifty years hence—a very sanguine estimate—the working-classes will have realized the striking economy of a vegetarian diet. Will not the Socialists have also made their mark by then, and rendered the continued acceptance of starvation-wages an impossibility? We have often read in the columns of *Justice* the emphatic and satisfactory assurance, *"It moves."* This being so, why should Socialists be troubled if Vegetarianism is seen to be moving also, and is it not possible that they are both moving towards the same end? That is a righteous indignation which denounces those so-called philanthropists who take upon themselves to recommend a vegetable diet to the working-classes while they themselves continue to eat flesh meat three or four times a day; but, indignant as we may be at the bad taste not to say hypocrisy of these officious advisers, it is scarcely fair to describe such persons as "Vegetarian Capitalists." Capitalists they probably are, but they cannot be Vegetarians until they have themselves adopted the vegetarian diet. The truth is that Vegetarians do not pretend that their system can offer a complete solution of the social difficulty, but only that it is an important accessory consideration. Still less have they the bad taste to preach Vegetarianism as a gospel exclusively designed for the poor, the whole point of their contention being that it is good for rich and poor alike. Those Socialists who imagine that the economic advantage of Vegetarianism is the only argument that can be brought forward in its favour, are therefore lamentably ignorant of the *raison d'etre* of Food Reform. I am not at present concerned to discuss the merits of Vegetarianism; but it may be well at least to point out on what grounds it is advocated by those who practise it.

First, it is indisputable that a great pecuniary saving may be effected by the total disuse of flesh-meat; and this, though not the only or most important aspect of Vegetarianism, is perhaps the most obvious in its bearings on questions both of national and individual interest. Food-thrift, like temperance, puts so much additional power into the hands of those who are willing to practise it. When therefore a capitalist advises his *employés* to adopt a vegetarian diet, it is possible that, intentionally or otherwise, he is suggesting a course which is more favourable to their interests than to his own. If socialist workers were to give a trial to Vegetarianism, and found that they were as strong, or stronger, in health, and much better off in pocket, their change of diet would be a distinct gain to the Socialist cause. But Vegetarians appeal not only to our pockets, but to our sense of justice and humanity. They may, of course, be mistaken in this appeal; and it may be very foolish to condemn the slaughter of innocent animals as brutal and inhuman; yet, whatever some persons may say of this kind of "sentiment," Socialists are scarcely in a position to ignore it, since by so doing they cut away the ground from under their feet, one of their own strongest arguments being itself based on this same sense of justice and humanity. When a Socialist sets aside the plea for humanity to the lower animals as a mere fad and crotchet, a Vegetarian might well retort that if the promptings of gentleness and mercy are deliberately disregarded in the case of the animals, it cannot suprise us if they are also excluded from consideration in those social questions where the welfare of human beings is concerned. If those who live selfishly on the labour of others are rightly denounced as "blood-suckers," do not those who pamper a depraved appetite at the expense of much animal suffering deserve a somewhat similar appellation? Then again there is the question of good taste which must, sooner or later demand our attention, even when all the capitalists have been driven out and a socialist *régime* is established. No community possessed of true refinement will tolerate such degrading and disgusting institutions as the slaughter-house and the butcher's shop, both of them a disgrace to civilization and decency. Here, then, is another point of view which may give socialists pause, before they jump to the conclusion that Vegetarianism is altogether a craze and hallucination. Lastly, Vegetarians assert that the simplicity of a Pythagorean diet is far more conducive to sound bodily health than the habit of flesh-eating; and in this assertion they are, to a great extent, borne out by Sir Henry Thompson's opinion, that "more than one half of the disease which embitters the middle and latter part of life among the middle and upper classes of the population is due to avoidable errors in diet." Here, once more, is an aspect of the food question which deserves the attention of Socialists, as of all thoughtful people. Is it not possible that even a Socialist community might suffer from these same "avoidable errors" in diet, when it enters on that period of general festivity and unlimited jollification to which some Socialists seem to look forward? It may be that when we have dethroned the capitalist and possessed ourselves of the good things which he now unjustly enjoys, we may still find ourselves exploited and rack-rented, even under a Socialistic Government, by such uncompromising landlords as indigestion and gout; and I greatly fear that disease is a capitalist with whom even social-democrats will find it difficult to contend successfully. For these reasons it is conceivable that food reform is a subject of more importance than some socialists are at present willing to admit.

This objection to anything that savours of food-thrift is sadly impolitic and short-sighted, being based on a total misconception of what such frugality really implies. The economy that almost of necessity accompanies a vegetarian diet is very far from being the same thing as niggardly parsimony or churlish asceticism. On the contrary, it is quite compatible with the most open-minded liberality, and the frankest cheerfulness. It is the golden mean between asceticism on the one side, and wastefulness on the other; and is simply the recognition of the fact that Nature's gifts to men are too bountiful and holy to be either slighted or squandered. Simplicity of diet is found by those who make trial of it to be the pleasantest as well as the most economical method of life; "plain living and high thinking" being no mere empty formula, but the expression of a very important truth.

The Thoreauvian and humanitarian views expressed in this article are logical extensions of positions Salt had taken by 1885 when he left Eton, and they point to the next phase of his work: humanitarian reformer and biographer and critic.

NOTES

1. Henry S. Salt, *Seventy Years Among Savages* (London: George Allen & Unwin, 1921), p. 74.

2. Salt to S. A. Jones, April 12,1890, Jones Collection, University of Illinois at Urbana-Champaign. All letters from the Jones Collection cited in this book are published with permission.

3. Salt, *Seventy Years Among Savages,* p. 76.

4. W. J. Jupp, *Wayfarings: A Record of Adventure and Liberation in the Life of the Spirit* (London: Headley Brothers [1918]), p. 120.

5. *Pall Mall Gazette*, April 28, 1888 (clipping from Salt/Pontin collection; page number missing).

6. Salt, *Seventy Years Among Savages,* p. 75.

7. For an account of warring factions among socialist groups, see E. R. Pease, *The History of the Fabian Society* (London: Frank Cass, 1963); Peter d'A. Jones, *The Christian Socialist Revival 1877–1914* (Princeton, N.J.: Princeton University Press, 1968); Stanley Pierson, *Marxism and the Origins of British Socialism* (Ithaca, N.Y.: Cornell University Press, 1973); A. M. McBriar, *Fabian Socialism and English Politics 1884–1918* (Cambridge, Eng.: Cambridge University Press, 1962); Warren Sylvester Smith, *The London Heretics 1870–1914* (New York: Dodd, Mead, 1968).

8. H. M. Hyndman, *The Record of an Adventurous Life* (New York: Macmillan, 1911), p. 307.

9. Archibald Henderson, *George Bernard Shaw: Man of the Century* (New York: Appleton-Century-Crofts, 1956), p. 216.

10. The *To-day* article is more easily available in H. S. Salt, *Literary Sketches* (London: Swan Sonnenschein, Lowrey, 1888), p. 39–58.

11. *Ibid.,* p. 58.

12. Pease, *History of the Fabian Society,* pp. 26–32. See also W. H. G. Armytage, *Utopian Experiments in England 1560–1960* (London: Routledge and Kegan Paul, 1961), pp. 327–41.

13. Pease, *History of the Fabian Society,* p. 26.

14. *Ibid.,* p. 30.

15. Henderson, *George Bernard Shaw,* p. 212.

16. Havelock Ellis, *My Life* (Boston: Houghton Mifflin, 1939), p. 282.

17. Bernard Shaw, *Fabian Tract No. 41* (London: Fabian Society, 1892), pp. 3–4.

3

Henry Salt: Humanitarian

"The purpose of the Humanitarian League . . . was to proclaim a
general principle of humaneness. . . ."

Seventy Years Among Savages

By 1891, Henry Salt was developing a world view which
embraced socialism, vegetarianism, and several other causes.
Humanitarianism was the name he used for this philosophy,
which was based on the principle that "it is iniquitous to
inflict unnecessary suffering on any sentient being." The idea
for creating a society to further such a philosophical world
view originated with Howard Williams, whose *Ethics of Diet*
had helped change Salt's life, and in 1891 a small group of
like-minded people assembled in London to inaugurate the
Humanitarian League. In the manifesto sent out into late-
Victorian England, which had no particular desire for such a
message, it was asserted "that much good will be done by the
mere placing on record of a systematic and consistent protest
against the numerous barbarisms of civilization—the cruelties inflicted by men on men, in the name of law, authority,
and traditional habit, and the still more atrocious ill-
treatment of the so-called lower animals, for the purpose of

'sport,' 'science,' 'fashion,' and the gratification of an appetite for unnatural food."[1]

Salt and the humanitarians were calling for "the emancipation of men from cruelty and injustice" and for "the emancipation of animals."[2] They knew that the movement would have little popular appeal and that its main support would come from vegetarians, who had two journals already circulating in England; from zoophilists, represented by the Royal Society for the Prevention of Cruelty to Animals; and from the several societies devoted to antivivisection.

The aims of the League were to be furthered by two journals edited by Salt: *Humanity,* later renamed *The Humanitarian* (1895–1919), and *The Humane Review* (1900–1910). Salt wrote hundreds of thousands of words for these two journals, and also produced during these years a steady stream of pamphlets on vegetarianism, the rights of animals, and other related subjects. In addition, he carried on the more tedious tasks necessary for the functioning of the organization; he wrote his American friend and fellow Thoreauvian Dr. Samuel Arthur Jones in 1893 that while others helped the League, "no one else has the time or inclination to do the *continuous* secretarial and organising work which is quite indispensable to the society's existence."[3]

The League gained much public attention with the publication in 1892 of Salt's *Animals' Rights,* a clearly written, scholarly study which started with the premise that animals, as well as men, should be "exempt from any unnecessary suffering or serfdom" and should have "the right to live a natural life of 'restricted freedom,' subject to the real, not supposed or pretended requirements of the general community."[4] Salt argued that the two major causes of the denial of animals' rights were the "religious" belief that animals have no souls and the Cartesian view that animals have no consciousness. Salt the classicist and rationalist is evident in the first chapter as he contrasted traditional Christian attitudes toward animals with Buddhist statements on the sacredness of all life and with the views of Seneca, Porphyry, and Plutarch, who "took still higher ground in preaching humanity on the broadest principle of universal benevolence."[5]

Having established his philosophic principle, Salt then devoted separate chapters to "The Case of Domestic Animals," "The Case of Wild Animals," "The Slaughter of Animals for Food," "Sport, or Amateur Butchery," "Murderous Millinery," "Experimental Torture," and "Lines of Reform." He drew his examples from classical and modern literatures and from his serious study of Victorian culture. For almost all of the next three decades the topics he had chosen for discussion in *Animals' Rights* were discussed in his journals, thus putting on public record in England many of the grossest cruelties of Victorian and Edwardian society.

Salt refused the easy answers. For example, to those apologists for hunting, he wrote: "As for the nonsense sometimes talked about the beneficial effect of those field-sports which bring men into contact with the sublimities of nature, I will only repeat what I have elsewhere said on this subject, that 'the dynamiters who cross the ocean to blow up an English town might on this principle justify the object of their journey by the assertion that the sea-voyage brought them in contact with the exalting and ennobling influence of the Atlantic.' " The chapters are filled with statements reflecting a Thoreauvian passion and commitment: "The sports of hunting and coursing," Salt says in the chapter on "Sport, or Amateur Butchery," "are a brutality which could not be tolerated for a day in a state which possessed anything more than the mere name of justice, freedom, and enlightenment."[6]

His passions were particularly strong in "Murderous Millinery" as he attacked the "reckless barbarism which has ransacked, and is ransacking, whole provinces and continents, without a glimmer of suspicion that the innumerable birds and quadrupeds which it is rapidly exterminating have any other part or purpose in nature than to be sacrificed to human vanity, that idle gentlemen and ladies may bedeck themselves . . . in borrowed skins and feathers."[7] As naturalist and conservationist, Salt was to point out in the following years the serious consequences to society of despoiling areas of natural beauty and of senselessly slaughtering animals and birds.

The torture and killing of animals in scientific experiments was the object of Salt's greatest scorn. The scientific mind, he insisted, believed in preserving rare birds by shooting and stuffing them. Scientists, he stated, could not study without killing, and vivisection was the logical outcome of the scientific method then holding sway. The key paragraph in his argument puts forth his own ethical and moral principles: "Nothing is necessary which is abhorrent, revolting, intolerable, to the general instincts of humanity. Better a thousand times that science should forego or postpone the questionable advantage of certain problematical discoveries, than that the moral conscience of the community should be unmistakably outraged by the confusion of right and wrong. The short cut is not always the right path; and to perpetrate a cruel injustice on the lower animals, and then attempt to excuse it on the ground that it will benefit posterity, is an argument which is as irrelevant as it is immoral. Ingenious it may be (in the way of hoodwinking the unwary) but it is certainly in no true sense scientific."[8]

Salt concluded his book with a chapter on "Lines of Reform," in which he argued that the solutions to the problems he had raised were to be found both in education and in legislation. He pointed to the difficulty in providing a humanitarian education for children when parents and teachers maintained their anti-humanitarian views. In urging legislation, he knew that it would not in itself prevent cruelty, because legislation "follows, not precedes, the development of . . . moral sense. . . ."[9] His closely argued pamphlet was clearly designed to reeducate adults.

As Salt must have expected, *Animals' Rights* was subjected to repeated assaults. He summarized the opposition in *Seventy Years Among Savages*. Professor D. G. Ritchie in *Natural Rights* argued that though "we may be said to have duties of *kindness towards* the animals, it is incorrect to represent these as strictly *duties towards* the animals themselves, as if they had rights against us." Ritchie was joined by Monsignor John S. Vaughn, who believed that "beasts exist for the use and benefit of man." G. K. Chesterton concluded that Humanitarians restricted their vision and they tended "to touch fewer and fewer things." In the long-running controversy, much reported in Salt's humanitarian journals, both Chesterton and Salt proved themselves to be strong willed and witty. Salt took particular umbrage, however, at Chesterton's charge that the humanitarian view was narrow; he argued that, far from restricting their horizons, humanitarians took the broadest of possible views. It was his belief, though his views were not shared by Ritchie, Vaughn, or Chesterton, that animals' rights should be considered in relation to social progress.[10]

Salt was aided in the propagation of his ideas by a Miss Eddy of Providence, Rhode Island, who paid for an American edition of the book to be distributed free to libraries in the United States.[11] The League's funds were always insufficient, but Eddy and others often made it possible to publish special volumes such as this one.

From 1891 to 1895, the League's office was Salt's rooms on London's Gloucester Road. In those early years, when there was no journal for communication, Salt recruited those with similar interests into the organization and published pamphlets and books such as *Animals' Rights*. In 1895, the League opened an office on Great Queen Street, where it remained until it moved to Chancery Lane. With the move to Great Queen Street, the monthly journal *Humanity,* later called *The Humanitarian,* was begun and was published until 1919, when the League disbanded.

Salt's superior organizational ability is seen in the intricate structures he developed. He appointed special departments to deal with sports, criminal law and prison reform, humane diet and dress, education of children, and animals' rights; he found aggressive people to work in these departments, to prepare pamphlets, write letters to editors, and compose statements for the annual meetings of the League. He also founded in 1900 *The Humane Review,* a journal devoted to publishing long articles on humanitarian subjects. For this journal, he was able to get contributions from Shaw, W. H. Hudson, Edward Carpenter, Ouida, Sydney Olivier, R. B. Cunninghame Graham, Aylmer Maude, Clarence Darrow, and many others. The articles published in the journal were well written, serious essays that brought the League considerable intellectual prestige. The journal also published literary essays on Tolstoy, Shelley, Thoreau, De Quincey, and other writers who particularly interested Salt.

The League made use of endorsements by members of Parliament and divines, by such notables as G. W. Foote, president of the National Secular Society, and by a few literary figures such as Meredith and Hardy. Hardy, for example, wrote in 1910:

Few people seem to perceive fully as yet that the most far-reaching consequence of the establishment of the common origin of all species is ethical; that it logically involved a readjustment of altruistic morals, by enlarging, as a necessity of rightness, the application of what has been called "The Golden Rule" from the area of mere mankind to that of the whole animal kingdom. Possibly Darwin himself did not quite perceive it.

While man was deemed to be a creation apart from all other creations, a secondary or tertiary morality was considered good enough to practise towards the "inferior" races; but no person who reasons nowadays can escape the trying conclusion that this is not maintainable. And though we may not ar present see how the principle of equal justice all round is to be carried out in its entirety, I recognise that the League is grappling with the question."[12]

Most literary figures remained aloof, however; Salt wrote Joseph Ishill in 1930 that work with the Humanitarian League alienated him from literary people.[13] A few political figures and bishops supported the movement, but they were a small group indeed.

THE RIGHTS OF ANIMALS

In 1895, with the founding of *Humanity* and the opening of an office, the League entered into a much more active phase of its work. A part of its effort was an extension of concerns set forth in *Animals' Rights*. These five of its aims are all interconnected:

A more vigorous application of the existing laws for the prevention of cruelty to Animals, and an extension of these laws for the protection of wild animals as well as domestic.

Insistence on the immorality of all so-called "sports" which seek amusement in the death or suffering of animals. Legislative action in the case of the most degraded of such sports.

The prevention, by the encouragement of a humaner diet, of the sufferings to which animals are subjected in cattle-ships and slaughter-houses; and as an initial measure, the substitution of well-inspected public abattoirs for the present system of private butchery.

An exposure of the many cruelties inflicted, at the dictates of Fashion, in the fur and feather trade.

Prohibition of the torture of animals by Vivisection in the alleged interests of science. [14]

While the League was concerned with cases of cruelty to domestic animals, most of its efforts were directed toward the protection of wild animals. One of its major campaigns was against the institution of the Royal Buckhounds. Salt and the League were well aware that there were other sports just as cruel, but they decided to focus their efforts against tame deer hunting, using the Royal Buckhounds as their example. [15]

The League had great difficulty in calling its case against the sport to the Queen's attention. Her secretary refused to bring League grievances to her notice. The Home Secretary refused. The Prime Minister refused. The League then petitioned the Queen to allow the matter to be put before her, and the Home Office was thus forced to show her the documents. The difficulties experienced by the League were effectively publicized. Queen Victoria took no action, but the League knew, from a private letter, that she was opposed to stag hunting. This information was published after her death, and as Salt notes "settled the fate of the Buckhounds."[16]

The campaign against the Royal Buckhounds took several forms. Memorials signed by prominent citizens were sent to the government. For example, in 1896, the headmaster of Rugby, the Archbishop-Designate of Canterbury, the Bishop of Hereford, and several MPs signed a letter to the Marquis of Salisbury asking that the government, headed by Lord Salisbury, take action. The petition was based on the following premises:

> There is little need to point out the unworthy nature of the park stag-hunt, for it has been repeatedly shown that the sport involves unfair treatment of the quarry, and merciless riding of horses in the effort to "save the deer for another day."
>
> We think that such a pastime is the reverse of creditable to those who indulge in it, and that it is calculated to check the growth of humane feeling in all who witness it, particularly the young. If the sport were carried on by a private pack, it would exercise this influence; much more then must this be the effect of the sport when it is conducted in the Queen's name and at the cost of the nation.[17]

The League was enormously aided by the stupidity of the pro-Buckhounders, who made statements about the "kindness" of the hunters in attempting to save the deer for another hunt; the League gleefully seized upon such statements and held them up to public scorn. The pro-Buckhounders published "an imaginary interview with the famous stag [called] Guy Fawkes, in which he was represented as hugely enjoying the chase."[18] But the interview was not published until three weeks after the stag had been spiked and disemboweled. The League turned that ineptitude to good account.

The entire campaign against the Royal Buckhounds took ten years, but once the battle was won Salt wrote that the victory of the small Humanitarian League "taught . . . high-and-mighty paid officials, and other hangers-on of the Hunt, a much deserved lesson that will not readily be forgotten." A Conservative Government had been forced to discontinue an institution which had lasted seven hundred years.[19]

The Royal Society for the Prevention of Cruelty to Animals did not take a public stand on the issue, and Salt, in explaining why, throws a great deal of light on the socially acceptable reform societies:

Mr. John Colam, for many years Secretary of the Royal Society for the Prevention of Cruelty to Animals, . . . had a great reputation for astuteness. Wily he certainly was, with the vast experience he had acquired in evading the double pressure of those who cried "forward" and of those who cried "back"; and he was a veritable Proteus in the skill with which he gave the slip to any one who tried to commit him to any course but the safest. He used privately to allege the backwardness of his Committee as a cause for this seeming timidity; thus he told me in 1901, when the fate of the Royal Buckhounds was hanging in the balance, that the R.S.P.C.A. was unable to take any public action, not from any remissness on his part, but because certain members of the Committee were afraid of alienating subscribers, including King Edward himself. Personally I liked Mr. Colam; he was humane so far as his interests permitted, and when one had realized, once for all, the uselessness of attempting to bind him to any fixed purpose, it was instructive to have an occasional talk with him. . . .[20]

Salt and those who worked with him in the League were generally outsiders and tended to follow their own consciences, unlike those Respectables such as Colam who chose to compromise their beliefs.

After the Royal Buckhounds had been abolished, Salt commented in a poem:

THE DEER DEPARTED

An Elegy

By a follower of the late Royal Buckhounds, on the King's Deer shot at Swinley Paddocks, April 12th, 1901, when the Hunt had been abolished.

> Alas, poor Deer! what cruel hand
> Thy life has thus cut short?
> Plague on the faddist crew that bann'd
> Our pleasant harmless sport!
>
> No more uncarted at the Meet,
> The proudest of the proud,
> Thou'lt frolic through suburban street,
> Pursued by Cockney crowd;
>
> No more, where grassy banks invite,
> By some sweet railway-side,
> The friendly playful hounds will bite
> Raw pieces from thy hide;
>
> Nor to thy cart, so snug and warm,
> The huntsmen will convey
> Thy precious blood-besprinkled form,
> "Saved for another day."

But I, who loved thee—by thy grave
   I linger broken-hearted,
And sing this sad funeral stave
   To mourn my Deer departed.

Didst wonder, since my love was such,
   I hunted thee so sore?
I could not love thee, Deer, so much,
   Loved I not Hunting more.[21]

The Eton Beagles

Salt, in an article entitled "Sport as a Training for War,"
maintained that sports and war were alike in perpetuation of
aggressiveness. He believed that "Sport is, in truth, a form of
war, and war is a form of sport. . . ," and that boys trained in
sports at Eton were indeed "future stalwarts of Imperialism."[22] But he did not believe that Eton boys would be good
soldiers merely because they had been trained in sports, for
sport "breeds the aggressive and cruel spirit of militarism, it
does *not* furnish that practical military training which is
essential to successful warfare. Sport may make a man a
savage; it does not make him a soldier."[23]

One of the League's longest-lasting sport controversies was
with Eton College, which, unlike other public schools, kept a
pack of beagles and engaged in hare-hunting. Salt, who both
loved and hated Eton, found in the hunt a subject which was
easily dramatized and which drew a tremendous amount of
public attention. From the *Eton College Chronicle,* written by
the boys of the college, Salt transcribed some of their accounts

of hare-hunting. These two schoolboy descriptions of the hunt are typical of the dozen or so that Salt published in a Supplement to *Humanity* for May of 1897:

"Tuesday, February 2nd, the Beagles met at Salt Hill. This was a real red-letter day in the annals of the E.C.H. . . . It was simply owing to the number of hares that hounds were deprived of blood, which they so much deserved."

"Thursday, February 4th, saw the Beagles at Dorney village. We started by drawing the ploughs the far side of Dorney, and before we got to the end of the first field a hare got up. . . . On hounds getting on the line again, they went at a screaming pace along the Dorney Brook into Dorney Court, where hounds pulled her down dead beat in the garden. Time, 1 hr. 5 min. This was the best and most satisfactory run we have had this Half, and may the E.C.H. have many more like it."

Salt argued that schoolboys need not be encouraged in cruelty and that boys could get necessary exercise without indulging in sports which depended on torture and suffering.

In 1902, the Humanitarian League sent a memorial to the Governing Body of Eton College protesting beagling, but the Governing Body decided not to interfere in the matter. The League then wrote Dr. Edmond Warre, the headmaster, asking that the hunt, which often ended with the "breaking up" of the hare, be changed to a drag-hunt. In a drag-hunt, a person pulls across the terrain a woolen stocking filled with aniseed, which gives out a strong scent. The beagles follow the scent just as if it were a stag, fox, or hare. The pace can be controlled, and farmers do not have their crops trampled and their domestic animals frightened. The League letter ended by noting that both the provost and the headmaster were members of the Windsor chapter of the Royal Society for the Prevention of Cruelty to Animals, the parent organization of which had stated that the Eton Beagles were "contrary to the principles" of the Society.

Warre, in his reply, gave the League excellent material to bolster its arguments. He insisted that terms such as "breaking up" were merely sporting expressions, unfortunately used by the boys in the school paper as they described the hunt, and that such terms did not imply anything more than that the hares were devoured by the beagles. The League then called to Warre's attention the many descriptions written by the boys of hares being subjected to prolonged chases and to torture by exhaustion, and the accounts of hares being severely mauled before being killed.

Warre insisted that it was improper for the League to infer that hunting demoralized the youth of the country, and he was unwilling to interfere "with the liberty which from time immemorial the boys have enjoyed in this matter." The League responded that it was not charging the Eton boys with conscious cruelty; it was more pointedly charging that the sport itself was cruel and demoralizing.

Warre acknowledged his membership in the Windsor branch of the RSPCA; but, he said, he "had never been given to understand that that society has condemned the hunting of wild animals," and, he added, if that were the policy of the Society, it should be known. The League then referred Dr. Warre to the RSPCA's journal for March of 1902, which condemned the Eton Beagles as contrary to the principles of the Society.

Having been bested in the argument, but in no mood to

compromise or change the custom, Warre declined to say more on the subject. The correspondence was published in part or in whole in *The Times, Standard, Morning Leader,* and other papers, drawing much public attention to the controversy. The RSPCA, however, insisting it had no control over elections in local societies, refused to take any action to remove the provost and Dr. Warre from their positions in the Windsor chapter of the Society. Salt then scathingly denounced the local chapter for not complying with the stated policy and also the parent organization for not taking action against the defiant Windsor branch.[24]

Salt participated in a satiric venture aimed at beagling in 1907 when he published two issues of *The Beagler Boy,* the stated purpose of which was to "save a gallant school sport from extinction." Salt knew that the absurdity of the articles would be apparent to the general reader but "would escape the limited intelligence of schoolboys and sporting papers." Etonians were indeed enthusiastic, and the *Sportsman* found the paper "a publication after our own heart." *The Evening Standard,* commenting on the satire, suggested that some of the beagler boys might even be converted.[25]

Public opinion, Salt says in *Seventy Years Among Savages,* was against the Eton Beagles, but to no avail, for the Governing Body and the headmaster were not moved by public pressure. In fact, Salt speculated, a headmaster who decreed the end of the Beagles would probably not be maintained in his position.[26]

Salt had known for decades that reform at Eton was wellnigh impossible. Having won the public opinion battle but having brought about no change, Salt, in one of his most caustic poems, borrowed and expanded a title from Gray:

FRAGMENT OF AN ODE ON THE EXTREMELY DISTANT PROSPECT OF HUMANE REFORM AT ETON COLLEGE

Say, Father Thames, for thou hast seen
    Full many a sprightly race
Blood-sporting on thy margent green
    The paths of beagling trace;
Who foremost now, with glad halloo,
The draggled quarry loves to view
    Dead-beat and circling vainly round?
Who most, for boyish pastime's sake,
Delights the mangled hare to "break,"
And "blood" the ravening hound?[27]

SLAUGHTERHOUSE REFORM

Salt was an ardent believer in vegetarianism, but the Humanitarian League included nonvegetarian members, and its official policy, in calling for a more humane diet, was designed to embrace the sentiments of both groups. In its crusade for the abandonment of private slaughtering and the substitution of public abattoirs, which would use more humane methods of slaughter and would be more sanitary, the League broadened its base of support, for the cleanliness of the shambles was a concern of vegetarian and meat eater alike. The League began public agitation on this issue in 1895, and it vigorously publicized both cruel methods of slaughter and the conditions of filth in many abattoirs. It also exposed the unsanitary condition of cattle boats which brought animals from Ireland and other countries for slaughter in England.

The League also protested the Jewish method of ritual

slaughter. A League member, Charles Forward, in an address in January of 1897, described Jewish slaughtering of animals as "a survival from barbaric times." His major objection was to the prolonged suffering inflicted on the animals during the long length of time used in preparing them for killing. While denouncing the Jewish religious practice, *Humanity* continued its call for a more humane diet, pointing out that a vegetarian diet would make slaughter of animals, both Jewish and Christian alike, unnecessary.[28]

Humanity published many articles on Jewish slaughter, and the League was pleased that the 1904 report of the committee appointed to consider the Humane Slaughter of Animals also condemned the Jewish method. But, as Salt wrote in *Seventy Years Among Savages,* almost twenty years later: ". . . nothing has yet been done to carry the recommendations of that Committee into effect, the supposed sanctity of a 'religious' usage having been allowed, as usual, to outweigh the clearest dictates of humaneness."[29]

When the League was ended in 1919, an unsigned "Retrospect" (undoubtedly by Salt) in *The Humanitarian* declared that the efforts of the association had helped bring about some changes on the cattle ships and in the shambles. That the job was unfinished was clearly understood, for Salt did not delude himself into thinking that League campaigns had established a utopia on this earth.

THE FUR AND FEATHER TRADE

The Humanitarian League's campaign against the fur and feather business was outlined by Salt in his chapter on "Murderous Millinery" in *Animals' Rights.* In the journals he edited, he continually pointed out that many species of birds were endangered because of the dictates of fashion. He often used irony and ridicule, as when he noted that the Duchess of York wore an aigrette when giving out prizes at an RSPCA meeting in 1895. He had come to a social view of the problem, one which would hardly win wide support: "As long as there are so many feather-headed women (and men), there will be little consideration of egrets, or indeed for any living being in whose exploitation there is any chance of profit, ornament, or pleasure."[30]

Seals, too, were threatened with extinction, and the League protested their wanton slaughter and the methods used—the seals were often skinned alive. The League argued effectively that more stringent laws were needed to protect wild animals and birds used in the creation of fashionable dress. This campaign was consistently of a high order, with well-written, logical articles pointing out the problem and possible solutions; *The Humane Review* published "The Fate of the Fur Seal" in Volume III and "The Plumage Bill" in Volume X. Salt printed many short articles in *The Humanitarian,* but it was a cause with few victories. Fashions have changed and vast numbers of feathers are not used nowadays on women's hats, but seals and alligators and many other species are still slaughtered for fashion.

A Lover of Animals AND VIVISECTION

Shaw's preface to *The Doctor's Dilemma,* much indebted to ideas of Henry Salt and to the causes espoused by the Humanitarian League, provides some helpful glosses for Salt's own play, *A Lover of Animals:*

[H]e who cuts your inside out receives hundreds of guineas, except when he does it to a poor person for practice.

Doctors are just like other Englishmen: Most of them have no honor and no conscience. . . .

Let us . . . not [shrink] from the fact that cruelty is one of the primitive pleasures of mankind, and that the detection of its Protean disguises as law, education, medicine, discipline, sport and so forth, is one of the most difficult of the unending tasks of the legislator.

On one occasion I was invited to speak at a large Anti-Vivisection meeting in the Queen's Hall in London. I found myself on the platform with fox hunters, tame stag hunters, men and women whose calendar was divided, not by pay days and quarter days, but by seasons for killing animals for sport. . . . The ladies among us wore hats and cloaks and head-dresses obtained by wholesale massacres, ruthless trappings, callous extermination of our fellow creatures. . . . We sent our sons to public schools where indecent flogging is a recognized method of taming the young human animal. Yet we were all in hysterics of indignation at the cruelties of the vivisectors. . . . I made a very effective speech, not exclusively against vivisection, but against cruelty; and I have never been asked to speak since by that Society. . . .

"Preface on Doctors," *The Doctor's Dilemma.*

Salt turned to playwriting to advance humanitarian causes; his first effort was a one-act play called *A Lover of Animals* which was originally printed in *The Vegetarian Review* in February, 1895, and was reprinted in Volume V (1904–5) of *The Humane Review.* The play shows that Salt had observed his friend Shaw's playwriting methods carefully. Also, Salt's subject matter may well have influenced Shaw's *The Doctor's Dilemma* (1906). Both writers made certain borrowings from the character of Edward Aveling, the notorious socialist. Both knew Dr. Aveling and Eleanor Marx well. Salt said of Aveling in *Seventy Years Among Savages:* "It is easy to set him down as a scoundrel, but in truth he was an odd mixture of fine qualities and bad; a double-dealer, yet his duplicities were the result less of a calculated dishonesty than of a nature in which there was an excess of the emotional and artistic element, with an almost complete lack of the moral. The character of Dubedat in Mr. Bernard Shaw's play, *The Doctor's Dilemma,* in some ways recalls that of Aveling, for nearly everyone who had dealings with him, even those who were on the friendliest of terms, found themselves victimized, sooner or later, by his fraudulence in money matters."[31] Dr. Kersterman in Salt's play is characterized as being a scoundrel in financial matters, as was Dubedat. Salt wrote *A Lover of Animals* before Eleanor Marx's suicide; long after her death, Salt wrote of her: "There was real tragedy . . . in Aveling's alliance with Karl Marx's daughter; for Eleanor Marx was a splendid woman, strong both in brain and in heart, and true as steel to the man who was greatly her inferior in both, and who treated her at the end with a treachery and ingratitude which led directly to her death."[32]

Salt does not comment on the genesis of *A Lover of Animals,* but Grace Goodheart may well be a combination of Eleanor Marx and Salt himself. In Salt's plot, Grace escapes romantic entanglement with Dr. Kersterman; Eleanor Marx, many of her friends thought, should have escaped from romantic entanglement with Dr. Aveling. Salt allows his heroine a Thoreauvian disengagement which Eleanor Marx was unable to achieve. Grace was, of course, a Thoreauvian just as Salt was, and she left a disagreeable job, just as Salt did.

A Lover of Animals was advertised for twopence in the April, 1895, issue of *Humanity.* The play was performed at St. Martin's Town Hall, on March 21, 1900. The performance, with amateur actors, was well received by the three hundred members of the audience, which included Mr. and Mrs. Shaw.

The drama, as printed in the February, 1895, issue of *The Vegetarian Review,* and reprinted in Appendix A, states clearly and amusingly Salt's position as an antivivisectionist and as a believer in the rights of animals.[33] Obviously written for propagandistic purposes, *A Lover of Animals* is nevertheless filled with paradoxical situations and humorous lines. It is, though, not of the same literary quality as Shaw's message plays.

When Shaw wrote his own play about doctors in 1906, he drew from some of the same sources Salt had apparently used, including the Aveling–Eleanor Marx relationship and humanitarian views held in common with Salt, but Shaw also made major use of the tragic early death of Jim Joynes in 1893. Shaw wrote Archibald Henderson in 1905 that Joynes "was slaughtered by a medical treatment so grossly and openly stupid and ruinous that I have never forgiven the medical profession for it since." He elaborated on that statement in the preface to *Salt and His Circle,* insisting that, when Joynes's heart failed and the doctors immobilized him and prescribed whiskey, they murdered him, and "This began my feud with the doctors, who are doing that still."[34]

Shaw uses the unseen character of Jane Marsh, who lost an arm because of Ridgeon's use of Koch's tuberculin, in much the same way Salt uses Pate, who was an idiot after brain surgery. Mrs. Hacket's belief that Pate was trepanned "for the sake of the students of the hospital, not for his own benefit at all" is a view of the medical profession also found in *The Doctor's Dilemma*.

Salt had been writing against vivisection for many years before he wrote *A Lover of Animals,* and Shaw clearly knew of Salt's earlier antivivisection writings in *Humanity* and in *Animals' Rights.* Shaw's play itself is not overtly concerned with antivivisection, but his preface, added in 1911, reflects the views of the Humanitarian League and may well have been influenced by Salt's play. Shaw wrote Salt in 1910: "The preface to the Doctor's Dilemma contains my final and complete utterance on Vivisection. It is barbarous enough to gratify even your thirst for the blood of respectable men."[35] Shaw's preface might properly be considered a brilliant summation of major positions adopted by the Humanitarian League.

CRIMINAL LAW AND PRISON REFORM

"A thorough revision and more humane administration of the Criminal Law and Prison system, with a view to the discontinuance of the death penalty and corporal punishment, and an acceptance of the principle of reclamation instead of revenge in the treatment of offenders"—"Aims and Objects" of the Humanitarian League.

One of the most effective League campaigns, for which a special department was established, was for the reform of criminal law. Sentences were not equal, and prison discipline was harsh and brutal. The League attempted "to humanize both the spirit of the law and the conditions of prison life, and to show that the true purpose of imprisonment was the reformation, not the mere punishment, of the offender." Salt enlisted many able people in this campaign. Dr. W. Douglas Morrison, the criminologist, led the League agitation which helped bring about the Prisons Act of 1898. W.H.S. Monck (Lex) worked for the establishment of a Court of Criminal Appeal and a revision of the Imprisonment for Debt law. Lex was an indefatigable writer of letters to editors, who often, as Salt remarked in *Seventy Years Among Savages,* made masterful use of irony.

In addition to organizing the various campaigns for reform of prisons and of criminal law, Salt wrote a one-act play entitled *The Home Secretary's Holiday* to advance his ideas. The play was performed for the League in May of 1902. It is a concise statement, touching on many aspects of Salt's views on the problem involved in reforming the criminal law and penal system. It is reprinted in Appendix B. A more sombre play than *A Lover of Animals,* Salt's second (and last) play is a presentation of several different criminological principles practiced and advocated in England at the beginning of this century.

Salt had a large store of information about prisons from his reading and from conversations with former prisoners who visited him in the League office. He wrote Edward Carpenter this account (presented in a slightly different form in *Seventy Years Among Savages,* with the *damned* and the hint of homosexuality removed) of an encounter with Oscar Wilde's warder:

I had a talk yesterday with ex-warder Martin, late of Reading Prison, and he told me some good things. He was Wilde's warder, and had evidently been chummy with him; in fact I suspect *that* was the "other reason" for his dismissal to which the Home Secretary darkly alluded. Here is one of his stories—Wilde complains to the chaplain of the darkness of his cell, pointing to the gloomy little sky-lights with some impatient remark that he could not see the clouds, &c "Oh, my friend," says the chaplain, "let me entreat you to desist from such thoughts. Do not let your mind dwell on the clouds, but on Him who is above the clouds, Him who—." "Get out, you damned fool," says Wilde, and out goes the chaplain and reports him, with the result—bread and water."[36]

The dark hints of homosexuality could not have been presented on the stage in those late-Victorian years, nor could the brutality of flogging, which Salt effectively used offstage. Even with the restrictions on the drama, would Salt have been a more effective reformer had he, like Shaw, concentrated his efforts on the theater? Would a play on prison reform with a run in the West End have been more effective than propagandistic articles in *Humanity?*

One of the major opponents of the League's views on prison reform was William Tallack, the secretary of the Howard Association, itself an organization for prison reform. Like the secretary of the RSPCA, he did not enjoy taking stands on principles. Salt says Tallack was out of sympathy with newer styles of prison reform. In Salt's play *The Home Secretary's Holiday,* Tallack is presented as Mr. Prim, who sees "segregation," "introspection," "self-questioning," "remorse," as means by which the convict may come to a realization of his guilt.[37]

Salt, though he had literary skills, produced only one-dimensional characters in the play, undoubtedly because he wanted his ideas to be of major importance. But Sir Charles Windham, the Warder, Mr. Prim, and Lady Windham are never more than stock characters, though their lines are amusing. Sir Charles has had himself sent to prison in order to investigate conditions, but there is no indication that he is strong enough to bring about prison reform. Lady Windham can do no more than prate romantically about Thoreau and Carpenter, whose works she has read but obviously can not understand. Amusing it is at times, but a good play it is not.

Could Salt have learned to combine propaganda and art? Perhaps he did not feel he had the time to learn the craft of playwriting. Perhaps Shaw discouraged him. At any rate, Salt wrote no more plays.

Salt's accomplishments in prison reform, then, were largely those of organizer and editor of materials contributed by the many other able and committed reformers who supported the League in this cause. The detailed articles in Salt's journals were effective and influential, for his authors had mastered their subjects and pled most effectively for reforms. At a time when there was considerable public pressure to extend the use of the lash in prisons, the League fought vigorously against such proposals. The League was particularly concerned with ameliorating legislation, such as the Criminal Appeal Act and more humane laws concerning imprisonment for debt, and its efforts met with some success.[38]

FLOGGING

Salt reflected many of his own views on flogging in the poem "The Hymn of the Flagellomaniacs":

> As the miser craves for treasure
> As the drunkard craves for grog,
> So we crave for morbid pleasure—
> Something sentient to flog!

Give us juvenile offender,
  Truant oft from school or church,
Yet for prison cell too tender:—
  Ah! to brand him with the birch!

Give us gaol-bird past repentance,
  Brutalised too deep for that:—
Ah! to wreak on him the sentence
  Of the sanguinary 'cat'!

All the tortures—hanging, burning,
  Cropping, thumbscrew, boot, and rack—
Pale before our fevered yearning
  For the bare and bleeding back.

As the miser o'er his treasure,
  As the drunkard o'er his grog,
So we gloat with maniac pleasure
  O'er our joy of joys—to flog![39]

Salt was, as his poem shows, well aware of the psychopathic qualities inherent in the nature of the flogger. Parents and schoolmasters, judges and rulers, he wrote, "have felt that in wielding the rod they were discharging a religious obligation, and not, as might otherwise have been suspected, gratifying some very primitive instincts of their own."[40] In article after article, Salt examined the justification for flogging, and found all the reasons specious. He could find no disciplinary or pedagogical reasons for parents and schoolmasters to flog children. He was convinced that such punishment did not deter crime. His own view was that "corporal punishment . . . is an outrage on what should, above all things, be held sacred—the supremacy of the human mind and the dignity of the human body."[41] All his activities against flogging proceeded from that premise.

The campaign of the Humanitarian League against flogging produced some limited improvement. Reform of parents and schoolmasters was probably not significant, but it was somewhat easier to see changes in the Royal Navy. The League's case was strengthened when officials of the Royal Navy quibbled, insisting "there was no 'flogging' in the Navy, for 'flogging' meant infliction not of the birch but of the 'cat.' " That blunder helped the League gather public support, and in 1906 the Navy did discontinue "birching," but as Salt noted in 1921, "the use of the cane, to the discredit of the Admiralty, is still permitted and defended."[42]

In 1904 Salt decided to use prose satire in his attacks against inhumanity, and published one issue of *The Brutalitarian: A Journal for the Sane and Strong.* The journal was "to be the official organ of those who hold, with the late Mr. G. W. Steevens, that 'we have let brutality die out too much.' It is full time, in this age of decadent humanitarianism, that some trumpet-tongued protest be raised against the prevalent sentimentality. . . ." The paper supported imperialism, flogging, blood sports. The printers had many requests for copies, but the press was cautious, suspecting that Chesterton or Shaw had perpetrated the satire. Salt felt that the venture helped the humanitarian cause, for the laughter produced by the praise of flogging temporarily stopped requests for more flogging. The proponents of such punishment, Salt noted, "did not relish their own panacea, when it was served to them in an undiluted form, and with imbecility no less than brutality as its principal ingredient."[43]

Though he helped bring about some needed reforms, Salt realized that he lived in a barbaric society and that this most sensual of punishments would be extremely difficult to eradicate, for it was sanctioned by both state and religion.

OTHER LEAGUE OBJECTIVES

The League also had these "Aims and Objects":

The extension of the principle of International Arbitration, and the gradual reduction of armaments.

A more considerate treatment of subject races in our colonies.

Recognition of the urgent need of humaner education, to impress on the young the duty of thoughtfulness and fellow feeling for all sentient beings.

In occasional articles in the *Humanitarian* or *The Humane Review,* the League took up these causes, as well as several others such as noncooperation and civil disobedience (as advocated by Tolstoy, not Gandhi), hospital reform, and conservation of natural areas; but these were not major campaigns. The League was too small in numbers and too limited in budget to address itself to all the causes listed in its "Aims and Objects," and it had few supporters as Europe moved toward World War I and fewer still during the war. Salt objected to "violence and trickery masquerading as 'patriotism'" and to "the brutal spirit of hatred and persecution which the war engendered."[44] Few wanted to hear what he had to say. He was tired and dispirited. He wrote Edward Carpenter in 1918: "I have told the Committee that I must give up at the end of the year the editing of the Journal, and such other work as I am doing for the League. I feel that I must be free now—cannot be tied any longer by committee meetings or having to bring out the ever-approaching 'next number' of the *Humanitarian*."[45]

And, indeed, by 1919 the League itself had to be disbanded. Its members were old, but, more important, its views had been rejected by most societies during the holocaust of war, with its political hatreds, indiscriminate violence and cruelty, military despotism, and general barbarism. Salt, in the midst of this failure, struck a Transcendental note, for he himself had not abandoned his views on universal kinship: "The lesson of the past six years is this," he wrote in 1921. "It is useless to hope that warfare, which is but one of many savage survivals, can be abolished, until the mind of man is humanized in other respects also—until *all* savage survivals are at least seen in their true light. As long as man kills the lower races for food or sport, he will be ready to kill his own race for enmity. It is not *this* bloodshed, or *that* bloodshed, that must cease, but *all* needless bloodshed—all wanton infliction of pain or death upon our fellow-beings. Only when the great sense of the universal kinship has been realized among us, will love cast out hatred, and will it become impossible for the world to witness anew the senseless horrors that disgrace Europe to-day."[46]

NOTES

1. *The Vegetarian Messenger*, Jan., 1891, pp. 6–7; Henry Salt, *Seventy Years Among Savages* (London: George Allen & Unwin, 1921), pp. 121–23.

2. Salt, *Seventy Years Among Savages*, p. 122.

3. Salt to Samuel Arthur Jones, Oct. 15, 1893, Jones Collection.

4. Henry S. Salt, *Animals' Rights* (New York: Macmillan, 1894), p. 85. There were translations into Dutch, German, French, and Spanish of this book, originally published in 1892. In addition to the original edition, there were editions in 1899, 1915, and 1922.

5. *Ibid.*, pp. 2–3.

6. *Ibid.*, pp. 56, 57.

7. *Ibid.*, p. 66.

8. *Ibid.*, p. 78. For an excellent study of this subject, see Richard D. French, *Antivivisection and Medical Science* (Princeton, N.J.: Princeton University Press, 1975).

9. *Ibid.*, p. 98.

10. Salt, *Seventy Years Among Savages,* pp. 125–28.

11. Salt to Jones, Oct. 15, 1893, Jones Collection.

12. *The Humanitarian,* May, 1910, p. 35.

13. *A Group of Unpublished Letters by Henry S. Salt to Joseph Ishill* (Berkeley Heights, N.J.: Oriole Press, 1942), p. 13.

14. *The Humanitarian* published a page of these "Aims and Objects" in many of its issues.

15. Salt, *Seventy Years Among Savages,* p. 152.

16. *Ibid.,* pp. 152–53.

17. *Humanity,* Dec., 1896, p. 173.

18. *The Humane Review* II (1901–2), p. 180.

19. *Ibid.,* pp. 178–80.

20. Salt, *Seventy Years Among Savages,* pp. 161–62.

21. H. S. Salt, *Consolations of a Faddist* (London: A. C. Fifield, 1906), p. 9.

22. H. S. Salt, *Killing for Sport* (London: G. Bell and Sons, 1914), p. 152.

23. *Ibid.,* p. 155.

24. The entire correspondence surrounding the Eton Beagles was published in *The Humanitarian,* June, 1902, pp. 25–27.

25. Salt, *Seventy Years Among Savages,* pp. 175–76.

26. *Ibid.,* p. 154.

27. Salt, *Consolations of a Faddist,* p. 25.

28. *Humanity,* March, 1897, pp. 21–22.

29. Salt, *Seventy Years Among Savages,* p. 150.

30. *Humanity,* Aug., 1896, p. 141.

31. Salt, *Seventy Years Among Savages,* p. 80.

32. *Ibid.,* p. 81.

33. Henry Salt, "A Lover of Animals," *The Vegetarian Review,* Feb., 1895, pp. 52–63.

34. Dan H. Laurence, ed., *Bernard Shaw: Collected Letters: 1898–1910* (New York: Dodd, Mead, 1972), p. 490; Shaw, preface to Stephen Winsten, *Salt and His Circle* (London: Hutchinson, 1951), p. 11; Archibald Henderson, *George Bernard Shaw: Man of the Century* (New York: Appleton-Century-Crofts, 1956), p. 800.

35. George Bernard Shaw to Salt, Sept. 27, 1910, Humanities Research Center, University of Texas at Austin, and Henry W. and Albert A. Berg Collection, The New York Public Library, Astor, Lenox and Tilden

Foundation (cited hereafter as University of Texas and Berg Collection). The original is in the Berg Collection.

36. Salt to Edward Carpenter, July 7, 1897, Carpenter Collection. See the published version in Salt, *Seventy Years Among Savages*, pp. 181–82.

37. Salt, *Seventy Years Among Savages*, pp. 139–42.

38. *Ibid.*, pp. 139–45.

39. Salt, *Consolations of a Faddist*, p. 28.

40. Salt, *Seventy Years Among Savages*, p. 137.

41. Henry S. Salt, *The Case Against Corporal Punishment* (London: Humanitarian League, 1912), p. 29.

42. Salt, *Seventy Years Among Savages*, p. 138.

43. *The Brutalitarian*, Oct., 1904, p. 1; Salt, *Seventy Years Among Savages*, pp. 174–75.

44. Salt, *Seventy Years Among Savages*, p. 220.

45. Salt to Carpenter, July 31, 1918, Carpenter Collection.

46. Salt, *Seventy Years Among Savages*, p. 246.

4

Henry Salt: Man of Letters

"I have written books because I *liked* doing so. . . ."
Salt to Joseph Ishill

LITERARY CRITIC

Henry Salt's approach to literature was that of a sympathetic interpreter trying to make the life and works of writers
intelligible to the reader. The writers who most appealed to
him were those concerned with the problems of society, those
with humanitarian interests. Salt was a free man, his simple
economic needs met by his annuity, and he was not account-
able to any educational institution or business official, nor to
any school of criticism—only to his own conscience. He was
free to support the causes in which he believed and to write on
subjects which interested him.

His bibliography was a long one, including biographies,
critical studies, poetry, translations, and autobiographies. In
his biographies and critical studies, which make up a large
part of his publications, he was most satisfied and successful
when he treated authors with whom he had the most sympathy, as in his studies of Shelley and Thoreau. He greatly
admired De Quincey's style and wanted to present the
humanitarian side of the writer. A naturalist himself, Salt was

attracted to Richard Jefferies, though he found Jefferies less appealing than Thoreau. He was less in sympathy with James Thomson (who signed his work B.V.), and since he was writing an "official" life, he had less freedom than in his other books. As a result this biography is inferior to his other literary criticism. The one author he wrote about with whom he was almost totally out of sympathy was Tennyson; it was Tennyson's traditional thought that Salt objected to. Salt was an astute observer of his society, and his examination of Lord Tennyson's thought was provocative. It is unfortunate that he did not turn his attention to other Victorian and Edwardian writers whose reputations were unduly large and needed deflating.

After his fall from Respectability, the course of Salt's writing was soon established, as his articles of the 1880s on Shelley, Thoreau, Thomson, De Quincey, and Tennyson show. His socialist-humanitarian point of view was already developed, and, while he refined his ideas in the years which followed, his approach to life and literature remained basically unchanged.

Shelley

It is a minor miracle that Salt was a devotee of Shelley, for his introduction to the poet occurred at Blackheath Preparatory School, when he was given a stanza of "The Cloud" for translation into Latin verse.[1] A task which might have led him to detest the poet permanently was instead the origin for his love of Shelley. Salt said in *Company I Have Kept,* "To me, Shelley has always appeared as one of those great poets who, like great mountains, if rightly viewed and approached, can give strength and comfort to mankind. The things which I love best of all in English poetry are Milton's *Lycidas,* that gem of perfect art, so rapturously beautiful to the ear, and certain passages and lyrics in Shelley's *Prometheus Unbound,* not less beautiful to the ear and still more beautiful to the heart."[2]

At Eton, Shelley was in bad repute. When a bust of the poet was proposed, the headmaster, J. J. Hornby, would not allow it, because Shelley "was a bad man."[3] Hornby regretted, Salt says, that Shelley had not attended Harrow instead of Eton. While Salt was a master at Eton, he read a paper on Shelley at the Ascham Society and discovered that few of the masters had any acquaintance with Shelley's poetry; most of them agreed with Hornby that Shelley was a disgrace to the institution.

Shelley's prose and poetry clearly helped introduce Salt to free thought, socialism, vegetarianism, and unconventional views on sex and marriage. Shelley was not the only influence on Salt in these matters, but he was one of the earliest and most important ones, and Salt did some of his best criticism on Shelley. His first full-length study of the poet was *A Shelley Primer,* published for the Shelley Society in 1887. The *Primer,* based on Salt's wide reading of Shelley scholarship, made use of the prefaces and notes from the major editions of Shelley's poetry and all the major biographical and critical studies, including Dowden's *Life of Shelley,* which had appeared the year before. Salt was writing for the general reader, for one who needed basic information on the poet. He began by sketching the "State of England in Shelley's Lifetime," concentrating primarily on the strong popular movements which followed the Declaration of Independence in America and on the stern reprisals which followed the Revolution in France.

In spite of repression, Salt pointed out, the ideas embodied in Paine's *Age of Reason,* Godwin's *Political Justice,* and Mary Wollstonecraft's *Vindication of the Rights of Women* were not successfully stifled.

Salt then turned, in a chapter on "Shelley's Life and Character," to a brief sympathetic sketch of the poet. He went to great pains to defend Shelley's character, noting that, by accepted standards of morality, Shelley's opinions and actions were reprehensible, but that, when seen from Shelley's point of view, they were justifiable. Salt recognized the unworldly qualities of the poet, but he pointed out Shelley's love and generosity, his impatience with authority and tyranny, and his gentleness. His chief fault, Salt argued, was his inclination, especially in his early years, to put forth doctrines in quarters where they had no chance of being accepted.

Salt then dealt in a straightforward way with "Shelley's Opinions": his atheism, which Salt believed was really pantheism; his views on morality and love, on social and political change; and his views on literature. Salt was attempting to present Shelley's ideas, opinions, and philosophy in the most sympathetic fashion.

After a brief chapter on Shelley's "Literary Characteristics," Salt summarized and evaluated the major poems and the prose works, giving a large amount of factual information and a sympathetic understanding of the works themselves. He ended with a bibliography and a section on "Shelley's Influence on Literature and Thought."

As a primer, the book is now out of date because of the immense amount of scholarship on Shelley since 1887, but for its time, it was an extremely useful little volume. Moreover, Salt's sensitive concern for the literary qualities of

Shelley's poetry and prose, and his insistence on seeing the poet as both artist and pioneer of reform, have a more contemporary than Victorian appeal. The volume still has historical interest, and it has been reprinted recently by Kennikat Press.

Salt's next large work on Shelley was *Percy Bysshe Shelley: A Monograph* (1888); in it, unlike many biographers of Shelley, Salt was neither hostile nor indifferent, but sympathetic and generally unapologetic. Leigh Hunt excepted, most of Shelley's biographers, Salt believed, did not approve of Shelley's social and moral views, no matter how much they admired his character and artistic genius; therefore, Salt concluded, they did not do justice to Shelley's ethical creed. Salt—freethinker, socialist, vegetarian—felt himself in complete sympathy with Shelley and therefore set out to write not a biography but a life sketch. He did not concentrate on the controversial matters normally of interest to biographers; rather, as he proclaimed his method in the preface, he would make judgments on what to accept and what to reject in the accounts by Hogg, Peacock, Medwin, and Trelawny. It was his intent to present what Shelley referred to as "a general image" of a character.

The sketch of Shelley is in a way serene, as it proceeds in undeviating fashion toward Salt's goal: to show Shelley, charged with a sacred mission, as if coming from another planet "to denounce and expose the anomalies that exist on this terrestrial globe, . . . the glaring contrast between might and right, law and justice, ephemeral custom and essential piety."[4] He sees Shelley as the advance guard of a future social state: "a prophet and forerunner of the higher intellectual development, a soul sent on earth before its due season by some strange freak of destiny, or rather, let us say, by some benignant disposition of Providence."[5]

The monograph was given a highly laudatory review in *Justice* on February 25, 1888; but *Justice* was edited for socialists, and more conventional critics were less convinced. Salt quotes one critic who accused him of making "an impudent endeavour to gain the notoriety of an iconoclast amongst social heretics with immoral tendencies and depraved desires." Such an attack convinced Salt he was on the right track, and so did praise from Lady Shelley, daughter-in-law of Shelley. Salt quotes in *Seventy Years Among Savages* a letter Lady Shelley wrote in 1888, probably after the publication of the monograph, speaking for herself and Sir Percy Shelley: "For the last thirty-five years we have suffered so much from what has been written on Shelley by those who had not the capacity of understanding his character, and were utterly ignorant of the circumstances which shaped his life, that I cannot refrain from expressing our heartfelt thanks and gratitude for the comfort and pleasure we have had in reading your paper." She also wrote Salt, "It is a great happiness for me to know, in my old age, that when I am gone there will be some one left to do battle for the truth against those whose nature prevents them from seeing in Shelley's beautiful unselfish love and kindness anything but evil."[6] Later, as Salt wrote Samuel Jones in 1894, Lady Shelley invited him for a visit, and he said he would probably see her "as she might show me records of importance."[7] Salt did not record the visit in his autobiographies, but it may well have taken place.

Percy Bysshe Shelley: Poet and Pioneer, published by William Reeves in 1896 and reprinted by Watts & Co. in 1913 and by George Allen & Unwin in 1924, represented Salt's mature judgment on Shelley. It incorporates, in a revised form, much of the 1888 monograph, and it is set in a framework clearly delineating the method and approach being employed. Salt started with the assumption that he should not attempt to retrace the steps of Dowden in biography or Forman in textual matters, but that he should carefully sift contradictory evidence and try to present a clear picture of the poet. Salt saw his role as that of "interpreter," for, he believed, "Sympathy alone can make his writing intelligible to us."[8]

The thesis was stated succinctly:

Against . . . the orthodox and sentimental view of Shelley there remains now to be set the rational and scientific one, the view which has all along been held by a handful of sympathisers, but has only begun within recent years to attract any considerable share of attention. According to this newer estimate, Shelley was the poet-pioneer of the great democratic movement; he anticipated, in his own character and aspirations, many of the revolutionary ideas now in process of development. We do not assert that he was a faultless being, that he was free from eccentricities and foibles, or that he did not share some of the intellectual errors of his time; but we do say that his outlook, far from being that of a weak-minded visionary, was, in the main, an exceptionally shrewd one, inasmuch as all the chief principles which were essential to his creed are found to have increased enormously in importance during the years that have passed since his death.

We hold that this philosophy of Shelley's must be considered together with, and not apart from, his poetry, that the two are inextricably connected and interwoven, and that Shelley the poet is to a large extent unintelligible, when dissociated, as he is still commonly dissociated, from Shelley the pioneer.[9]

After the introductory chapter, "Rival Views of Shelley," Salt included the revised material from the 1888 monograph and then added two new chapters: "The Poet" and "The Pioneer." In "The Poet" Salt defended Shelley against his detractors and argued for the interrelationship of poet and prophet:

a genuine liking for lyric poetry is a gift that is innate in a man and cannot be acquired by study—it is either there or not there from the beginning, and it is either there or not there to the end; so that there are doubtless many students of Shelley, among all classes of his readers, whether revolutionists or the contrary, who miss much of what is most subtle and impalpable in his verse. But I will assert that, where this lyrical sense is present, the man who understands Shelley as a pioneer will understand him the better, not the worse, as a poet. The reader who most fully sympathises with the ideas that underlie the polemical rhetoric of *Queen Mab* will also most fully sympathise with the soaring raptures of *Prometheus Unbound*.[10]

In "The Pioneer" Salt forcefully presented Shelley's views on religion, political and economic reform, and sexual and dietary questions. He concluded with a positive, Transcendental-Thoreauvian view that, though it might take years or even centuries, Shelley's "splendid vision of the ultimate regeneration of mankind" would be fulfilled. Salt shared almost totally Shelley's humanitarian and social views, and Salt's belief in the eventual triumph of Shelley's idealism was an affirmation of his own optimistic world-view.

Percy Bysshe Shelley: Poet and Pioneer remains a significant approach to the understanding of Shelley. It would be a mistake to claim too much for it, since Salt was using nineteenth-century biographies and inadequate texts; but the emphasis on Shelley as *both* poet and pioneer is convincing and useful, pointing, as it does, toward contemporary studies of Shelley such as Gerald McNiece's *Shelley and the Revolutionary Idea.*

Salt was a prominent member of the Shelley Society, which was founded by Dr. F. J. Furnivall in 1886, and included among its most noted members W. M. Rosetti, Buxton Forman, and Shaw. The Society called much public attention to the poet through its meetings and discussions and through its publications and its facsimile reprints of rare Shelley items.

In *Seventy Years Among Savages,* Salt noted that most of the members of the governing committee of the Society admired Shelley's artistic genius but were "unaware of the conclusions to which his principles inevitably led, and of the live questions which any genuine study of Shelley was certain to awake." When G. W. Foote, president of the National Secular Society, spoke to the Society on Shelley's religion, most of the members of the committee, Salt says, "marked their disgust for the lecturer's views, which happened also to be Shelley's, by the expedient of staying away."[11]

According to the extensive account in *Seventy Years Among Savages,* the Society staged the first performance of *The Cenci,* which had to be performed privately after the license for a public performance was refused. Salt felt that this performance was the Shelley Society's greatest achievement. Certainly *The Cenci* created a sensation and was widely reviewed.

Salt and Shaw, and a few other radicals, propagandized for a view of Shelley quite different from the general attitude of most Society members. It was Shaw who said at a general meeting of the Society, on January 26, 1887: "Like Shelley, I am a Socialist, an Atheist, and a Vegetarian."[12] In another instance, radicals were aided by W. M. Rosetti, when he threatened to resign because a majority of the committee wanted to refuse the membership application of Edward Aveling, whose alliance with Eleanor Marx was similar to Shelley's liaison with Mary Godwin. Aveling was admitted, but Salt recognized that the Society had been placed in an "absurd and impossible position."[13]

Salt was firm in his view of Shelley as a pioneer reformer, and his position was clearly strengthened by a letter from Eleanor Marx in 1892 in which she spoke of the "enormous influence" of Shelley upon the Chartists. She wrote, "I have heard my father and Engels again and again speak of this; and I have heard the same from the many Chartists it has been my good fortune to know. . . ."[14]

In *Seventy Years Among Savages,* Salt ended his account of the Society with two brief anecdotes. After the fashionable members left the Society, it continued to meet at University College, Gower Street, with only five or six members attending, including a Mrs. Simpson, who was always present. Though the old lady was well liked, for she was a humanitarian and a Shelleyan, the members were embarrassed "when her filial piety prompted her to give us copies of her father's writings, a bulky volume entitled *The Works of Henry Heavisides.* It was a sobering experience to become possessed of that book, the title of which conveyed a true indication of the contents."[15] Salt meant his readers to see that the Society was moribund. Only anecdotes were left. The second story is more irreverent. At the Shelley Centenary (August 4, 1892), which was marked in Horsham by a meeting of London gentlemen and Sussex squires come to praise Shelley, one speaker orated on the poet's "shining garments . . . so little specked with mire." Salt reported that Shaw later convulsed an audience with a description of the Horsham apologetics and then published an account of the meeting suggesting that Shelley should be represented on a bas-relief at Horsham "in a tall hat, Bible in hand, leading his children on Sunday morning to the church of his native parish."[16]

Salt's admiration for Shelley never wavered throughout his life; he constantly quoted Shelley in his writings and devoted long sections to the poet in his autobiographies. In his old age, he wrote Joseph Ishill that he had given up certain subjects such as wild flowers and certain authors he had once been devoted to, so that he might reserve himself "for the few really great ones (such as Shelley) who are ever in my thoughts." Mrs. John Davies, an old friend, was a frequent visitor during Salt's last years; she read Shelley to him throughout his last illness and up to the time of his death.[17]

James Thomson ("B.V.")

Salt's *The Life of James Thomson ("B.V.")* (1889, revised 1898) was undertaken at the request of Bertram Dobell, Thomson's friend and publisher. Both Thomson and Salt were Shelleyans, though Thomson was a pessimist and Salt was not. Salt should have been an ideal biographer of Thomson, for he had a sympathetic understanding of outcasts and unrespectables, but he was too much influenced by Dobell's views of the poet. Though Salt interviewed many people who knew Thomson, when the evidence was contradictory or puzzling, he followed Dobell's interpretation. For instance, though Salt was slightly wary of the story, he nevertheless overemphasized the death of Matilda Weller as a cause for Thomson's pessimism. Salt knew from his interview with Charles Bradlaugh that Matilda was a child of thirteen when she met Thomson and that stories of a betrothal were merely Thomson's poetical inventions. William Schaefer, in *James Thomson (B.V.): Beyond "The City,"* has demonstrated convincingly that Salt did not use the evidence before him to examine carefully this "love affair" but published instead the Dobellian interpretation. In addition, Schaefer shows that Salt had great difficulty in dealing with Thomson's alcoholism;[18] Salt (a teetotaler himself, though Schaefer does not mention this) even went so far as to speculate that Matilda's death fostered Thomson's drinking.

Salt's biography, then, though it contains much interesting factual material based on letters and interviews, was not a success, for Salt obviously slanted his account to fit the theses already developed by Dobell. In most respects, Salt's difficulties in this biography are those which have continually plagued "authorized" biographers.

Though Salt was not an objective biographer of Thomson, he did profit greatly from his intensive work on the poet. He came to realize that pessimism should take a rightful place in man's philosophy, for the knowledge that human efforts will fail could not be set aside. This melding of Thomson's pessimism with the optimism Salt took from Thoreau and Shelley clearly strengthened Salt's own understanding of the world.

Salt's researches for the Thomson biography also augmented his literary anecdotes. He interviewed one of Thomson's landladies, who could offer no help other than that her former lodger was dead, but she proposed that if Salt wanted to write the biography of "a good man, a real Christian, and a total abstainer" he should write about her dead husband. In another instance, Salt wanted to quote from a letter of Swinburne to W. M. Rosetti, a letter praising the poem "Weddah and Om-el-Bonain" (adapted from a love story which Thomson found in Stendahl's *De l'Amour*) as having "forthright triumphant power." Swinburne refused, saying that the praise was the result of "a somewhat extravagant and uncritical enthusiasm." Swinburne went on to attack Thomson for not leaving behind "a respectable and memorable name." Salt did not miss the irony of Swinburne's comments on respectability. He knew, from personal observation, that Swinburne's own critical judgments were completely dominated by Theodore Watts-Dunton, who explained that he had remarked to Swinburne: "I wish you would re-read that poem ["Weddah and Om-el-Bonain"] of Thomson's, as I cannot see that it possesses any great merit." A few days later, Swinburne replied, "You are quite right. I have re-read [it], and I find it has very little value."[19]

Thoreau

Salt's interest in Thoreau was long standing, and Salt was a major influence in bringing Thoreau to the attention of English readers. Only a few articles on the Concordian had appeared in England when Salt began to publish on Thoreau. After his first Thoreau essay in *Justice* in 1885 (quoted in Chapter 2), Salt set out to reach a wide general audience, placing an article on the poet-naturalist in the November, 1886, issue of *Temple Bar*. In this article, he noted the lack of a good biography, but he made careful use of much of the printed material on his subject. The collected works were not published until 1906, but Salt had read most of Thoreau's works then in print, as well as the memoirs or essays of H. A. Page, W. Ellery Channing, J. R. Lowell, Robert Louis

Stevenson, and Emerson. Salt began his article with a brief biographical sketch, then analyzed Thoreau's main philosophic ideas. He emphasized Thoreau's belief in "the perfectibility of man," his reverence for ancient philosophies and religions, his attempts to simplify life and to avoid luxuries, his individualism, and his humanitarian views. Salt stressed Thoreau the naturalist as well as Thoreau the social thinker, and he saw clearly the importance of the essay on civil disobedience.

Salt's 1886 essay is a remarkably well-informed work for one who had to rely on printed sources only and who had never been in the United States. Within three years, Salt was to begin expanding this essay into a book-length study. He did not wish to confine himself to published sources, and he began requesting information from those who had known Thoreau and from those who could provide him with records and memoirs. He wrote W. S. Kennedy on August 30, 1889:

My friend Edward Carpenter, whom I believe you know, tells me that he thinks you might possibly be able to give me some help towards a biography of Thoreau—I am working at a volume in which I wish to combine a clear and comprehensive account of Thoreau's life with a fuller and more serious estimate of his doctrines than those given in the existing memoirs. Mr. Harrison Blake has kindly promised to give me what assistance he can, and so have some other friends and students of Thoreau.

If you should chance to know of any out-lying sources of information, or unpublished letters, I should be very much obliged to you if you would tell me of them.[20]

The tone of the letter was one which would inspire confidence, and indeed Salt and Kennedy corresponded until Kennedy died in 1929.

Salt wrote Daniel Ricketson a somewhat more elaborate letter, setting out in greater detail his intention in the Thoreau biography. To an initial inquiry of Salt's, Ricketson had sent a copy of Thoreau's letter to Ricketson of February 12, 1859, on the death of John Thoreau, to which Salt replied:

Dear Sir,—I am exceedingly obliged to you for your kind letter and the copy of Thoreau's most interesting account of the death of his father. Let me first answer your question about my *modus operandi* in this volume on Thoreau which I am now preparing. My object is to give (1) a clear and succinct account of Thoreau's life, gathering up and arranging in their due order all the scattered records of him to be found in periodicals, as well as the information given by Messrs. Channing, Sanborn, and Page. (2) A fuller and more serious estimate of Thoreau's *doctrines* than any hitherto published, and a critique of his literary qualities. The book will consist of about ten or twelve chapters, the first two thirds of it being biographical and the remaining third critical. I shall aim throughout at *interpreting* rather than criticising in the ordinary sense, it being my belief that in the case of such a real man of genius as Thoreau it is the duty of the critic to accept him thankfully, and not to carp unduly at his limitations, though of course not shutting his eyes to them.[21]

He modestly told Ricketson in the same letter that "it has always been one of my desires to write a good life of Thoreau. It will be my own fault if I do not do this now, for I have received a great deal of kind help from America."[22]

Salt's attempts to gather new information were successful, and F. B. Sanborn, H. G. O. Blake, Daniel Ricketson, Dr. E. W. Emerson, Edward Hoar, Col. T. W. Higginson, Dr. A. H. Japp (H. A. Page), John Burroughs, W. S. Kennedy, and Dr. Samuel A. Jones were mentioned in the 1890 biography for having contributed to the study.[23] Salt was dependent on many Americans to supply the information not otherwise available in the British Museum Reading Room. In exchange Salt was helpful to American Thoreauvians. His letters to Samuel A. Jones indicate that he arranged for a secretary to copy articles for Jones, checked references in the British Museum Reading Room, sent on articles about Thoreau from English newspapers, and made great efforts to keep him posted on Thoreau's English reputation.

Ricketson, in sending the letter on the death of Thoreau's father, quite correctly observed that Thoreau's letters to friends would help explain the man. Salt had to rely largely on the 1865 Emerson edition of Thoreau's letters and on those letters which were published in memoirs and articles. He was also aware that not having access to Thoreau's unprinted journals was a serious handicap, and he wrote to Higginson: "I cannot hope to write a final Life of Thoreau, but I aim at showing the real solid aspects of his life and doctrines, so consistent and intelligible throughout, if men would only study them with sympathy and insight."[24]

Salt's biography of Thoreau was virtually completed by November of 1889, and on the twenty-eighth of the month he wrote the publisher Richard Bentley:

> I send herewith the MS of my Life of Thoreau.
>
> I have still to add to it some more papers promised me from America. Also I hope to get the letters addressed by Thoreau to the only Englishman who became well acquainted with him—a Mr. Cholmondeley, nephew to Bishop Heber. Otherwise, with the exception of a short appendix of bibliography, &c, the work is complete.

Of the letters I have inserted so far, the majority are cited from the volume published in Boston in 1865, and a few are unprinted ones.[25]

Bentley obviously read the manuscript quickly, for on January 6, 1890, Salt was writing the publisher that he was pleased to learn that the Thoreau manuscript was acceptable. Salt assumed that an edition of a thousand copies would be printed and that publication would be in the spring of that year. Within the next few months, Salt wrote Bentley about possibilities for distribution in the United States and about the portrait of Thoreau to be used as a frontispiece—the crayon drawing by Rowse was finally decided upon.[26]

The Thoreau biography had some favorable reviews. For example, *The Spectator,* after noting the faults of earlier biographers, said of the Salt study:

[Salt's] perception of motive and tendency is as marked as are his complete command and skilful grouping of facts. And his reading of ethical purpose is self-consistent and interesting. Here Thoreau stands, fair and complete amid his proper surroundings, for Mr. Salt has found local colour and aptly used it. He has been as industrious as he is devoted, and has left no stone unturned. He not only understands his subject; he seems to have gained identity with him through some kindredship of interest, opinion, and thought. And he is careful to avoid painting too much in bright colours, and so incur the charge of white-washing! He seldom puts his points too strongly, and is concerned to let Thoreau, as far as possible, speak for himself. While he does not agree with Mr. R. L. Stevenson that Thoreau, in a cynically-humorous way, sought to impose on himself no less than on his readers, as in the essay on "Friendship," he is prudent enough to admit that light may be thrown on

some of Thoreau's apparent paradoxes by perceiving that sometimes he half-humorously fenced his deepest thoughts, and only
expressed them by asides.[27]

Edward Carpenter wrote Mrs. Salt from Ceylon, "I read the
little Thoreau vol. with great interest on board ship. The
defence of John Brown is fine, and that paper throws great
light on his whole character. I hope H. will feel cheered up
about his work now, and not think it is all unprofitable, Eh!"
The biography was not published in the United States, and
Samuel Jones provided at least one reason in a letter to
H. G. O. Blake. Jones put the blame on F. B. Sanborn: "The
same creature told Mr. Salt, when in London, that he could
use his influence with Houghton Mifflin and Co. to secure the
publication of Thoreau'[s] Life in America, and in consequence Mr. Salt forwarded to him advance sheets of the book.
In Concord Library Mr. Sanborn showed me a letter frssh [sic]
from Mr. Salt thereupon, and added: 'I don't know about
urging the publication of this book, as it may hurt the sale of
my own.' "[28]

Unfortunately, Salt's Thoreau collection and his correspondence concerning Thoreau is in private hands and un-
available.[29] From the Journals of George Sturt, however, we can
learn one contemporary reaction. Sturt knew and admired
Salt, and wrote in his journal on November 16, 1890, before
he had finished the Thoreau biography: "A well-done book,
and entertaining. I am not quite sure, though, that I care for
biographies of such men as Thoreau: they are too apt to
suggest and insist upon a partial view of a whole man. But
Salt keeps himself well in the background, and is besides
vastly sympathetic:—to a certain degree; i.e. as far as he can

follow Thoreau." Upon finishing Salt's biography of Thoreau, Sturt wrote in his journal: "My respect for Salt is increased considerably. He takes what is to my mind a most just view of Thoreau. I felt at times a little quarrelsome, where a concession was made that 'perhaps' his was only a half-view of life, etc., etc.: but I am inclined to think this is Salt's knowing way of winning admirers for Thoreau. He is prepared to accept him unconditionally, to defend him through thick and thin, even though he takes lower ground than you ask. It follows that you on higher ground go yet further, and find yourself in the attitude desired by Salt, namely of defence of Thoreau's character."[30]

Once the volume was published, Salt began collecting materials for additions. Samuel Jones informed him that in following Sanborn he wrongly pictured John Thoreau as rather dull and Cynthia Dunbar Thoreau as a gossip. Salt wrote Ricketson for his opinion, and Ricketson replied that Sanborn had lived in the Thoreau household but that people had widely different perceptions of personality. Ricketson continued:

Although the portraits of Mr. and Mrs. Thoreau which you have copied from Mr. Sanborn are readily recognized, I should never have spoken of them in any manner that could have been construed into any disrespect for their genuine worth. Our philosopher was indebted undoubtedly to both his parents for much of his rare qualities—to the father for a calm, patient, industrious spirit, with great honesty of purpose and performance. . . . On the other hand, Mrs. Thoreau was an unusually active, voluble person, rather tall. . . . a great talker, and strong delineator of character, but not unlike many other good housewives gifted in relating historical and domestic events.[31]

Salt was convinced by the statements of Ricketson and Dr. Jones and made subtle changes in the 1896 edition to draw a more sympathetic portrait of the parents: Mr. Thoreau, in addition to being "quiet, plodding," became also "thoroughly genuine and reliable," and Mrs. Thoreau's humor changed from "shrewd keen" to "keen dramatic," and she was no longer "fond of dress and fond of gossip," though she still "often monopolized the conversation with her unfailing flow of talk."

In the 1896 edition (recently reprinted by Archon Books), Salt omitted many of the quotations "from the Letters, Diaries, Excursions, etc." which had been inaccessible to English readers in 1890. The basic plan of the biography was exactly the same, although he did incorporate new information, as noted above, and correct errors of fact such as his earlier statement that Thoreau's hut was a station on the Underground Railway. The 1896 edition was inscribed to Samuel Jones, and Salt's more than one hundred letters to him indicate a great indebtedness to Jones, both for his scholarly and bibliographic efforts and for his continued encouragement. Jones reciprocated by dedicating to Salt his collection of early articles on Thoreau, which he entitled *Pertaining to Thoreau.*

What is most noteworthy in the biography of Thoreau (both the 1890 and 1896 editions) is the sympathetic concern for Thoreau as a human being, as a writer, and as a social thinker. Salt was able to capture Thoreau's distinctive qualities but did not turn his back on Thoreau's perversities and failures: "His lack of geniality, his rusticity, his occasional littleness of tone and temper, his impatience of custom, degenerating sometimes into injustice, his too sensitive self-consciousness, his trick of over-statement. . . ." But Salt saw these failings as "incidental," not marring "the essential nobility of his nature." He clearly saw Thoreau's genius: "In an age when not one man in a thousand had a real sympathy with nature, he attained to an almost miraculous acquaintance with her most cherished secrets; in an age of pessimism, when most men, as he himself expresses it, 'lead lives of quiet desperation,' he was filled with an absolute confidence in the justice and benevolence of his destiny; in an age of artificial complexity, when the ideal is unduly divorced from the practical, and society stands in false antagonism to nature, he, a devout pantheist, saw everywhere simplicity, oneness, relationship."[32]

Salt seriously considered Thoreau's defects and character blemishes catalogued by Lowell, Stevenson, Emerson, and others, admitted those he judged fair but defended Thoreau when he found the attacks unjust. In the concluding paragraph of both editions, he observed: "We shall do wisely in taking him just as he is, neither shutting our eyes to his defects nor greatly deploring their existence, but remembering that in so genuine and distinctive an individuality the 'faults' have their due place and proportion no less than the 'virtues.' "

Salt read Thoreau with rare understanding; almost everything of his own—his humanitarian articles, his biographies, his pamphlets pleading for social justice, his autobiographies—is infused with a Thoreauvian spirit. Like Thoreau's, his audience was small. He wrote Samuel Jones on June 9, 1892, that the Thoreau volume had sold only eight copies the previous year. In 1895 when he wrote Bentley for permission to revise the Thoreau biography for inclusion in the Walter

Scott series, he noted, "I hope that a cheap edition may be the means of selling some copies of the original one. I am sorry, for your sake as well as my own, that the book fared so badly."[33] More than four decades later, Salt wrote Raymond Adams that the chief fault of the study "was the extreme deference" which he paid "to the authority of Emerson,"[34] but many scholars today agree with Walter Harding's estimate of it when he awards it high praise in *A Thoreau Handbook*.

Although Salt was and is largely ignored, his work on Thoreau is an enduring achievement of a man of principle writing about another man of principle. Salt wrote W. S. Kennedy in 1929 that he was revising his biography but unfortunately this revised edition was not published. His original work is still the most gracefully written, most sympathetic biography of Thoreau yet produced.

Though *Justice* did not review either the 1890 or 1896 biography of Thoreau, several of the various socialist groups were indebted to Thoreau and would naturally find a sympathetic biography of Thoreau useful. The Fellowship of the New Life publication, *Seed-time,* reflecting the philosophic grounding of the organization, made many favorable references to Thoreau. On a massive scale, Robert Blatchford in *Merrie England,* two million copies of which were sold, introduced vast numbers of readers to Thoreau. Blatchford began his book by urging his readers first to read *Walden,* and he liberally laced quotations from Thoreau into his book, largely in a call for the simplification of life and the throwing over of old values in search of a more "spiritual" life. Salt had serious reservations about Blatchford as a Thoreauvian; he wrote Samuel Jones on March 1, 1901, that Blatchford "has a great vogue among a certain section of working-men for a sort of serio-jocose journalistic style. . . . I do not like either his philosophy or his physiognomy."[35] Despite Salt's doubts about Blatchford's dedication to Thoreauvian philosophy, Blatchford did make Thoreau known to a different audience, and some of these new readers must have been curious enough to look into the cheap edition (1/6) of Salt's *Life of Thoreau* published by Walter Scott.

It is also possible to see how Salt's biography brought Thoreau to the attention of vegetarians. The English vegetarian publications in late Victorian times contained random mention of Thoreau, but in 1896 Howard Williams published a revised edition of *The Ethics of Diet: A Biographical History of the Literature of Humane Dietetics, From the Earliest Period to the Present Day,* with a chapter on Thoreau. Williams's influential book on vegetarianism was a bible for dietetic reformers; it was admired by Gandhi, and the first edition was translated by Leo Tolstoy. The Thoreau chapter was largely based on Salt's biography of Thoreau and on *Walden.* Williams gave a brief biographical sketch and praised "the force and originality" of Thoreau's character and writings. Williams did not maintain that Thoreau was a "pure" vegetarian; he noted that Thoreau did not absolutely renounce flesh foods, but was rather a follower of the "Natural Life," showing by example how to live "less conventionally and artificially." Williams quoted with praise several of Thoreau's statements on diet and diet reform, but he came to a conclusion which Salt would not have strayed into: If Thoreau had been properly "instructed in the philosophy of Dietetic Reform, he would have made it a question not only of the *future* destinies of the race but of the *present* and universal obligation."[36] It is difficult to imagine *who* could have successfully instructed Thoreau in diet. Salt understood Thoreau's individualism, as Williams did not. The chapter in Williams's book was important, however, because it did bring Thoreau to the attention of diet reformers. Salt himself made a better statement on Thoreau's dietary views and practices. In an article entitled "Thoreau" in the *Hygienic Review* for May, 1896, Salt, even though writing for vegetarians in a vegetarian magazine, did not take the easy way out. He described fully and accurately Thoreau's dietary habits and philosophy, and he did not apologize for Thoreau's lapses into meat-eating. He stressed Thoreau's independence of mind and his humane views. Salt's sympathetic presentation, even when he was writing in a special-interest journal, was characteristic of him. In the 1890s he wrote a series of literary articles in the *Hygienic Review*—articles on Anna Kingsford, Edward Carpenter, Thoreau, Shaw—which, while concentrating on the dietary views of his subjects, were consistently of a high quality and without the usual rhetoric of a special pleader.

Gandhi also is known to have been influenced by Salt's biography of Thoreau. During his student days in London (1888–91), Gandhi was dissatisfied with English food. He finally located a vegetarian restaurant; as he went in, he purchased a copy of Salt's *A Plea for Vegetarianism* (1886), which he read carefully. Salt's book began with a quotation from Thoreau: "I have no doubt that it is a part of the destiny of the human race, in its gradual improvement, to leave off eating animals, as surely as the savage tribes have left off eating each other, when they came in contact with the more civilised." Gandhi was convinced by the logic of the book, for he wrote in his *Autobiography:* "From the date of reading this book, I may claim to have become a vegetarian by choice."[37] Previously, he had merely followed orthodox Hindu dietary laws. Gandhi also read Howard Williams's *The Ethics of Diet,* though the edition he read did not have a chapter on Thoreau.

Gandhi had begun to play a part in the London Vegetarian Society, and on September 19, 1890, he was elected to the executive committee. He was a delegate, as was Salt, to the Conference of the Vegetarian Federal Union in May of 1891, and both Salt and Gandhi gave papers the second day of the conference.[38] The two men may have met at other times, since Gandhi was deeply interested in dietary as well as social reform during this period of his life.

Almost four decades later, on September 18, 1929, Salt wrote Gandhi:

You will hardly remember me; but I had the honour of seeing mention of my book, "A Plea for Vegetarianism," in a translation of your Autobiography, and I once saw you, I think, at the office of the Humanitarian League in London. On the strength of this, I am taking the liberty of writing to you.

Some forty years ago I published a Life of Thoreau, the author of that remarkable book, "Walden"; and an American friend of mine is now collecting material for a new and fuller Life, for which purpose I am handing over to him the various letters and press-notices that are in my possession. In the last letter which I received from this friend, Mr. Raymond Adams, of North Carolina, he asked me whether I thought that *you* had been a reader of Thoreau, and had been at all influenced by him, as on many subjects your views and Thoreau's seem rather akin. Not being able to answer his question, I told him I would venture to write to you direct and ask you. That is the cause of this letter.

I have been a vegetarian close on fifty years, and it has greatly benefited me, both in health, and in what is still more important, in spirit. I was much interested by what you wrote on the subject in your Autobiography.

With apologies for thus troubling you, I remain yrs. faithfully Henry S. Salt.[39]

Gandhi answered on October 12, 1929:

I was agreeably surprised to receive your letter. Yes, indeed your book which was the first English book I came across on vegetarianism was of immense help to me in steadying my faith in vegetarianism. My first introduction to Thoreau's writings was, I think, in 1907, or late[r], when I was in the thick of [the] passive resistance struggle. A friend sent me Thoreau's essay on civil disobedience. It left a deep impression upon me. I translated a portion of that essay for the readers of Indian Opinion in South Africa which I was then editing, and I made copious extracts from that essay for that paper. That essay seemed to be so convincing and truthful that I felt the need of knowing more of Thoreau, and I came across your Life of him, his "Walden" and other short essays, all of which I read with great pleasure and equal profit.[40]

The first mention of Thoreau in Gandhi's journal *Indian Opinion* was on September 7, 1907, but it is not known just when Gandhi first read "Civil Disobedience," *Walden,* and Salt's *Life of Henry David Thoreau*. It is clear, however, that Salt was a vital link in the transmission of information about Thoreau to Gandhi. Just as Salt's *A Plea for Vegetarianism* solidified Gandhi's "faith in vegetarianism," Thoreau's "Civil Disobedience" confirmed Gandhi's faith in passive resistance.[41]

Tennyson

Before his fall from Respectability, Salt had been a devoted reader of Tennyson. He knew *Maud* by heart and avidly sought news of the Poet Laureate from Kegan Paul, who was a friend of Tennyson. In the winter of 1878–79, however, Salt met Ruskin, who discoursed unfavorably on Tennyson; Salt regarded this conversation as one of the turning points in his life.[42]

Salt began to reexamine his views on Tennyson, and in the February, 1884, issue of *To-day,* he published "The Tennysonian Philosophy." Salt's views were quite like much twentieth-century criticism of Lord Tennyson's poetry; he admired the poetical powers of the poet laureate but found his philosophy "false and hollow." Following Ruskin, Salt attacked the jingoism of *Maud* and asked, "What are we to think of the moral teaching of a writer who was so carried away by the bellicose spirit of the time as to use all the resources of his art and poetical skill to vilify peace and glorify war?"[43]

Salt did not go so far as to charge that Tennyson pandered to the taste of Respectables, but he regarded the poet's writings as "representative": "One may find in his works the current theories and speculations of the age, stated with marvelous force and unexampled felicity of expression, but the man who, amid the din of conflicting creeds, seeks for moral or religious guidance and support, such as thousands have sought and found in the teaching of Carlyle and Browning and Ruskin, will look in vain for such assistance in the writings of the Poet Laureate."[44]

In 1890, Salt expanded his Tennyson essay for publication as a pamphlet entitled *Tennyson as a Thinker.* Though the basic ideas of the 1884 essay remained intact, Salt had refined his argument and made his points more tellingly. He began with James Thomson's damaging statement, "Scarcely any other artist in verse of the same rank has ever lived on such scanty revenues of thought as Tennyson."[45] Salt then argued against the inflated criticism which elevated Tennyson into the literary presence of Shakespeare and Milton. He praised Tennyson when he dealt with great and simple emotions in "Ulysses," "The Lotus Eaters," "St. Agnes' Eve," and a few other poems, but attacked the poems which were concerned with social controversy. Salt believed that Tennyson's leading principle was "law and order"; but, when orderliness was broken, Tennyson became "the most lawless and disorderly of men."[46]

From his own humanitarian-socialist position, Salt examined Tennyson's major poetry and found much of it wanting in thought; he felt that Tennyson's social philosophy had been determined by his birth, education, and social surroundings and that the poet "was quite incapacitated for recognising the progressive and intellectual tendencies of the times in which he lived."[47]

Robert Buchanan wrote to Salt saying that he was in agreement with much of what Salt said, but that his own friendly relations with Tennyson kept him from expressing his opinions, even after the death of the poet laureate.[48] Shaw held an even more caustic view of Tennyson than Salt did; he wrote Pakenham Beatty: "Brahms is just like Tennyson, an extraordinary musician, with the brains of a third rate village policeman."[49]

Salt's pamphlet caused a good deal of controversy. Much of the press took the view, Salt remembered, that it was Salt's own stupidity which brought him to such conclusions. Salt on Tennyson was admired by advanced thinkers and social outsiders but rejected by the Respectables.

De Quincey

Salt admired the prose works of Thomas De Quincey in much the same way that he respected the poetry of Shelley. He found De Quincey's style distinguished, and he pointed out that, though De Quincey was ostensibly a Tory, he was also a humanitarian, who spoke out against corporal punishment, prostitution, and women working in mines. In 1904 Salt published in Bell's Miniature Series of Great Writers a small book on De Quincey; the volume appeared just before Christmas and escaped press notice. It was particularly unfortunate that the volume was overlooked, because the study had many fine qualities. It is obvious that Salt had made use of the British Museum Reading Room and had read carefully all of De Quincey's works and all of the important criticism before he began his writing. The study, while it was a sympathetic account of De Quincey's life and work, did not ignore, nor overemphasize, the part opium played in his life. Salt stated his thesis simply and eloquently: ". . . what is especially praiseworthy in De Quincey, yet has not received one half of its due meed of praise, is that together with his high gift of imagination, great literary powers, and deep insight into that mystic part of man's nature which few other writers have fathomed, he was endowed with most tender human sympathies and a sensibility in some respects far in advance, not only of his own age, but of that in which we now make bold to pass our confident judgments on him, nearly half-a-century after his death."[50]

After a brief biographical chapter, Salt turned to a factual recording of De Quincey's works; in this section, he was offering to the general reader and student abstracts of De Quincey's major works. In the third chapter, Salt showed himself to be a sensitive critic, dealing with the visionary and imaginative qualities of the writer, with his style, and his concern for human suffering. This chapter is the best in the book, for in a limited space Salt caught the greatness and the weakness of the writer. The last chapter was again factual, a careful explication of *The Confessions of an English Opium-Eater*.

Though the book received no critical notice, it is not surprising that Emily de Quincey wrote Salt on May 18, 1907, that his book had completely captured her father. Miss de Quincey seemed little interested in the literary works of her father, or in Salt's literary judgments, but she was eager to write about her father as a person. She wrote nineteen long letters in all to Salt, the most significant sections of which he published in *Company I Have Kept*. (The letters are now in the Houghton Library at Harvard.) The letters show Miss de Quincey's belief that Salt had been able to see beyond the eccentricities of her father and to present him as he was. Salt had previously shown this power of sympathy in writing about Shelley and Thoreau. Salt's weakness, in the De Quincey study at least, was in attempting to combine in one brief book both biography and criticism. Had Salt decided to write a comprehensive biography, based on unpublished sources, his work would certainly be better known than it is now; instead he chose to stay with readily available published sources and to write what he hoped would be a "popular" book, widely read and likely to change popular misconceptions. In his own autobiographies, he did not express disappointment with his failure.

Richard Jefferies

After he left Eton, Salt became interested in Jefferies, and in 1894, four years after his Thoreau biography, he published *Richard Jefferies: His Life & His Ideals* (reprinted in 1905). An ardent naturalist himself, Salt felt a great affinity for Jefferies, who had also put aside orthodox religion and traditional social and economic views. In his brief study, Salt successfully traced Jefferies's development from a naturalist who enjoyed hunting and praised "the Great House" and its game-keepers—a stage Salt called "the rather rudimentary phase of the sportman-scientist, who may, or may not, develop into something better"—to the poet-naturalist in search of "ideal beauty," "physical perfection," and a more ample "soul life."[51] Salt skillfully put Jefferies in the tradition of Thoreau and Shelley.

Salt was again in sympathy with his subject, for he had himself made much the same intellectual journey, and he therefore argued for the superiority of Jefferies's later works over his earlier *The Gamekeeper at Home*. Salt presented his evidence carefully and perceptively; it is a model study which, decades after it was published, still helps readers understand Jefferies.

Salt seems to have enjoyed the controversy which developed over his skepticism about Jefferies's deathbed conversion to Christianity. Critics pointed out that Sir Walter Besant had testified to that conversion in his *Eulogy of Richard Jefferies*. Sir Walter, however, wrote Salt that the conformity was outward only: Mrs. Jefferies read the Gospel of St. Luke to her dying husband, and he was too weak not to acquiesce. Sir Walter further confided that Jefferies's views "never changed from the time that he wrote *The Story of My Heart*."

Sir Walter thought that Salt's skepticism about the conversion was well founded, but he justified his own version of the event because it gave consolation to the widow.[52]

General William Booth was particularly disturbed by Salt's reservations about Jefferies's deathbed conversion. "Infidelity," Booth wrote, "is not helped forward by falsehood." Even though Salt informed Booth of Sir Walter's comments, the general refused to withdraw his statement.[53] Throughout the controversy, however, Salt did not lose sight of the fact that it was not as a Rationalist but as a poet-naturalist that Jefferies would be remembered. Salt's book is successful in its delineation of Jefferies as poet-naturalist.

OTHER LITERARY WORK

Salt constantly made excursions to mountains and fields and wrote accounts of his nature studies which he collected in two volumes, *On Cambrian and Cumbrian Hills* and *The Call of the Wildflower.* He has been called "an English Thoreau," and his natural histories give good reason for such a designation.

Salt's training as a classicist was put to good use in his translation of *Treasures of Lucretius.* After he retired from active participation in the various humanitarian movements, he brought to completion his excellent translation of Virgil's *Aeneid,* published with the encouragement and financial help of Shaw.

His active interest in the ideas of Thoreau, Shelley, Godwin, Adams, and Barlas led him to edit selections from the works of these authors, for he wanted to present their works to a large general audience. He also edited poems of animal life, a reflection of his commitment to the rights of animals, and *Songs of Freedom,* which chronicled the development of the revolutionary ideal.

Salt was a successful autobiographer; his *Seventy Years Among Savages* remains an immensely useful and informative book about ethical, socialist, and humanitarian movements in the Victorian and Edwardian periods. His two memoirs of Eton are quietly evocative of that now-lost world. *Company I Have Kept* is thinner than the other autobiographies but contains many useful details about Salt and his friends.

Finally, Salt was an occasional poet who could celebrate friends and satirize the foibles of the world. In his poetry, as in his other literary work, he did not achieve popular success, though his critical notices were generally good, but Salt pursued his literary career serenely, for he believed in his own messages.

Books of Natural History

On Cambrian and Cumbrian Hills: Pilgrimages to Snowdon and Scawfell (1908, revised 1922) was written by an avid naturalist, obviously much indebted in style and approach to the nature writings of Thoreau. Salt was not intent upon writing a popular tourist guide or a technical book; rather, he wrote in an attempt to capture "a true expression of the love which our mountains can inspire." The first part of the book is indeed as descriptive, evocative, and meditative as Thoreau's own natural histories. Salt writes: "What, then, are the requisites for the pilgrim of the mountains? Two only: a strong purpose in his heart and stout nails in his boots. With these, and with no other guides than map, compass, and common sense, he may go his ways among the Cambrian and Cumbrian hills, and may see sights (if he be worthy to see them) which will make his memory the richer; and if he is wise enough to take but little baggage and live on simplest foods, to shun the hotel and make the cottage his resting-place, he will perhaps learn, if not the secret of the mountains, yet the secret of the mountaineer—the full and abiding happiness of the mountain life."[54]

In the chapter "Slag-Heap or Sanctuary?" Salt turned to a savage denunciation of those who were despoiling the mountains with their tunnels and mine buildings, who were discoloring the lakes with chemical wastes, poisoning the streams and the air, and killing or driving away the wild animals. With Thoreauvian passion he wrote:

The pretence that there is something selfish and anti-democratic in the desire to save our mountain scenery from destruction is absurd; on the contrary, it is entirely owing to its devotion to the fetish of "property" that the public has so long allowed these places to be exploited for private gain, and has stood by in utter apathy and indifference while a handful of speculators and traders have benefited at the expense of the community. Nor do we give to our mountains even that protection which other antiquities enjoy. What would be said if a Bill were submitted and passed in Parliament to authorize some private company to pull Westminster Abbey or Stonehenge to pieces and make a profit out of the ruins? It is no exaggeration to say that the Society for the Preservation of Ancient Monuments, familiarly known as "Anti-Scrape," would have the whole nation at its back in its resistance to such vandalism; yet a mountain such as Snowdon is a far more ancient monument than Stonehenge or the Abbey, and the vandalism which is now being successfully accomplished is of a still more insensate kind.[55]

Long before most conservationists were concerned, Salt had mounted a campaign to save the English countryside. His solution was to nationalize districts such as Snowdonia and to preserve them for the "use and enjoyment" of the people. His call for nationalization was not just the automatic socialist reflex; it was the result of Salt's serious thinking about ways to best preserve areas of natural beauty. His argument was a powerful one, expressed with great passion and rhetorical skill, and his volume was, he noted in *Company I Have Kept,* highly praised by John Muir, a leading American naturalist and conservationist.

The Call of the Wildflower (1922) shows Salt as a sensitive poet-naturalist, again following closely the example set by Thoreau. Explaining why his preference for the wild in nature was stronger than his regard for the domestic garden, Salt wrote, "A garden is but a 'zoo' (with the cruelty omitted); and just as the true natural history is that which sends us to study animals in the wilds, not to coop them in cages, so the true botany must bring man to the flower, not the flower to man."[56] His concern was not with the uses of flowers or the structure and analysis of flowers. What he desired was "a knowledge of the loveliness, the actual life and character of plants in their relation to man. . . ."[57] Salt was not a herbalist or a botanist; he was a man heeding the call of the wildflowers, and his approach was essentially Thoreauvian—he, too, wanted to know flowers as flowers.

Salt's intent, probably, was to do for wildflowers what W. H. Hudson had done for birds, and, indeed, *The Call of the Wildflower* is a solid achievement. It is both poetical and informative, with vivid descriptions of flowers in particular locations, from the coast of Sussex to the Welsh mountains and the northwest. Salt did not miss an opportunity to castigate those who destroyed wildflowers, both those who did so heedlessly by picking them in vast quantities and those who destroyed fields and meadows for profit as cities and factories encroached on the countryside. For all of his well-taken jeremiads against the destruction of flowers, Salt nevertheless appears as the gentle poet-naturalist-philosopher, with vast knowledge worn lightly, aware that much more is to be learned and observed.

In the chapter on Thoreau in *The Call of the Wildflower,* Salt began by quoting Emerson on Thoreau: "He was the attorney of the indigenous plants, and owned to a preference of the weeds to the imported plants, as of the Indian to the civilized man."[58] Using a term borrowed from Linnaeus, Salt called Thoreau a Botanophilist. Thoreau, though not a botanist, was intent on knowing flowers, of getting nearer to them. Salt captured the essence of Thoreau's attitude to wildflowers and explained, in his appreciation of Thoreau, much of his own approach. Salt was not a blind follower of Thoreau; rather, he had come to the same conclusions. Those who delight in Thoreau's nature writings will find Salt's books of nature studies particularly satisfying.

In *Our Vanishing Wildflowers,* published by Watts in 1928, Salt once again drew attention to the "insane greed of collectors" and to the motorist who stopped to pick, uproot, or trample bluebells, primroses, and cowslips. He showed great concern for the pollution of rivers and for the littering of gullies and peaks in the Lake District and in North Wales. He argued that contempt for Nature and natural life was one of the most disagreeable characteristics of modern man.

Translator

Salt was trained as a classicist, and as he grew older he did not break his ties with that part of his past. Virgil had appealed to him when he was in school, and he had translated parts of the Georgics for recreation. Vegetarian passages in Ovid had inspired him to make translations of those sections. Martial's epigrams were a great favorite, because Martial was the keenest of observers of "the humorous aspects of social life." Ramsay MacDonald published some of Salt's translations from Martial under the title "The Father of Epigram."[59]

Salt's first translation in book form was *Treasures of Lucretius: Selected Passages from the De Rerum Naturâ,* published for the Rationalist Press Association in 1912. He adopted as his model Milton's "Lycidas," that is, an irregular sequence of rhymed lines. Salt believed that blank verse was the best form for translation of Lucretius and Virgil, but he suggested that only the best poets could employ blank verse—others produced dullness.

Lucretius appealed to Salt because of the poet's concern for all suffering life and because of his hatred of superstition and tyranny. As Salt rendered Lucretius's central belief: ". . . the universe is ruled by wholly natural laws, and . . . mankind is free to work out his own destiny, undisturbed by any supernal guidance. With the same object of liberating us from the fear of the grave, he insists with deep earnestness that the soul dies with the body, and that the after-life, concerning which men so afflict themselves in anticipation, is but a fable and a dream."[60] Salt shared this belief.

Lucretius's views on death were of special interest to rationalists. "In the Lucretian philosophy," Salt wrote in the preface to his translation, "the conquest of death was to be achieved, not by denying its powers, but, on the contrary, by a full and frank recognition of its certainty and its endlessness. . . ."[61] The well-known passage on death which concludes the third book gives an indication of Salt's abilities as a translator, and it is a good example of the didactic nature of the poet's message:

> Why, then, doth danger's hour affright us so?
> By what false love of life are we misled?
> Since one sure term for mortals is ordained,
> The unfailing death which all must undergo.
> Still by the same old paths our way we wend,
> Though life itself no new delights can give;
> The joys we lack seem fairest; but, attained,
> We crave the more for others in their stead,
> As open-mouthed we ever thirst to live,
> Nor guess what fate the future may bestow,
> Nor when shall come the incalculable end.
>   E'en by long living we detract no jot
> From the great death-time, nor one hour can gain
> From those unnumbered years when we are not.
> Heap life on life till ages pass—'tis vain;
> For death eternal waits thee evermore.
> Nor for a briefer space shall he be dead,
> Whose light of life but yesterday hath fled,
> Than he who perished years on years afore.[62]

For many years, Salt worked at translating Virgil, though he never expected his entire translation to be published. Watts & Co. did print, in 1926, his version of Book IV, *The Story of Dido and Aeneas*, in which Salt again used the irregular sequence of rhymed iambic lines utilized by Milton in

"Lycidas." Shaw wrote Salt on September 14, 1926: "I agree about Virgil. Morris's long lolloping lines are out of character. Dryden is not varied enough, and too masculine. (Morris told me that Dryden was so close to the original as to be a first rate crib). I think you have solved the problem as far as it is soluble; and I find you readable for a longer stretch: in fact I went right through your bit at one go. If you will publish the whole I will finance it; and we can divide the profits half & half until I am paid off."[63] On October 3, Shaw wrote: "Get it ready for press as soon as you can; for tomorrow (or thereabouts) I die."[64] On January 13, 1928, he asked, in response to a letter of Salt's: "What will Vergil (ci-devant Virgil) cost? With sufficiently blasphemous notes you might induce the Rationalist Press to share the risk. It might begin a series of Atheist Classics. I do not wish to be indelicate; but as I am rather keener about your personal ease than about Vergil (who has, after all, a fair share of publicity from Dante and others) I shall not earmark the money. My alarmed imagination pictures 15 Sandgate Road [Salt's house] as a hovel."[65] Salt himself seems to have been totally unconcerned about the poverty in which he lived as he concentrated on the problems of a translator.

In *Company I Have Kept,* Salt referred at length to his correspondence with scholars after the publication of *The Story of Dido and Aeneas.* The vice-provost of Eton wrote him that the rhymed lines "read like blank verse, and yet there are echoes and answers, often from far away, which produce a lovely effect."[66] Others were less convinced. Professor J. W. Mackail felt the rhymed lines did not reproduce the effect of the hexameters and suggested that "Lycidas" was successful because it was "quasi-lyrical."[67]

Salt completed his translation of the entire *Aeneid* and sent it off to the Cambridge University Press on February 7, 1928. He wrote Shaw that day:

I have at last heard from the syndics of the Cambridge University Press. They do not respond to my suggestion that they should share in the expense of publication, but they will consider the question of publishing on commission. This, I believe, they only do when they are satisfied that the work will not do them discredit. They ask to see the complete manuscript; and I am today forwarding it. They will then send me an estimate. I will let you know when I hear from them definitely.

I daresay Watts & Co. would give a lower estimate; but probably the ability of the Cambridge Press to get [the] book to the right quarters would more than make up for that.[68]

The subvention was £189, which Shaw sent on February 14, 1928. The profits were to be divided as Shaw had suggested two years before. The book was well printed and designed, and the preface was gracefully written. The translation had good notices: *The Times Literary Supplement* called it "more readable . . . than any verse translation of Virgil since Dryden." The reviewer praised as "well justified" the use of irregular line sequences as in "Lycidas."[69] Salt wrote Joseph Ishill in April of 1930 that less than a hundred copies had sold the first year—merely three in America. Only a small group of scholars were interested, Salt said, and there were no general readers at all who could be relied upon to purchase his books.[70]

Salt's intentions in the translation are perhaps best seen in a letter he wrote to W. S. Kennedy:

There have not, as yet, been a great number of press-notices—, not more than half-a-dozen of any real importance—, but so far they have been on the whole very favourable, especially about the choice of metre, which they grossly acclaim as "the true formula." In several cases, too, they express the opinion that this is the best of the published versions.

I could hardly expect more than this, without being as unreasonable as some poets are! And I don't consider myself a *poet*; so that I by no means resent such (just) criticisms as that my verse is "always poetical, never poetry." I hope that some real poet, instead of adopting a *wrong* medium, as Dryden did, will some day use the right one, and produce a translation that is itself a poem. For I look on the Englishing of Virgil as, so to speak, a social task, not a merely individual one; in the sense that any one who attempts it should be glad if his successors can make use of his efforts and build something better thereon. That is how I feel, any how, about my own version.[71]

Anthologies

Salt edited many anthologies on subjects which interested him and which he felt should be brought to the attention of the general public. He selected his items carefully, and wrote brief, pertinent introductions.

In 1890, he published Thoreau's *Anti-Slavery and Reform Papers,* with an excellent introductory note emphasizing Thoreau's anarchism—"the claim for the individual man of the right of free growth and natural development from within—the same claim that has been advanced in other words by Whitman, and Tolstoi, and Ibsen, and William Morris. . . ."[72] In 1895, he published *Selections from Thoreau,* which contained extracts and essays covering the whole range of Thoreau's major work. His intent, as he wrote to Samuel Jones on March 8, 1894, was to bring Thoreau to the attention of a large audience and to increase Thoreau's reputation in England. He wrote Jones a week later that he was so eager to have such a volume published that he agreed to do the work even though he probably would receive no money at all for it.[73]

Salt also published in 1895, with F. B. Sanborn, Thoreau's *Poems of Nature,* but Sanborn was not reliable as an editor, and it is particularly unfortunate that Salt himself could not have traveled to America to work directly with the Thoreau manuscripts. Salt was aware of the difficulties, as he wrote to Jones: ". . . this sort of editing, without access to the original *MSS,* is poor work at best; I can only hope some will use the materials properly some day! What is wanted in all cases is what Thoreau wrote, not what his literary friends were good enough to write for him."[74] Salt's intentions were to produce a reading text, and he defended his punctuation of the Thoreau poems in another letter to Jones: "Each generation to some extent has its own method of punctuation, which renders bygone methods unintelligible. Thoreau seems to have gone in for almost unlimited commas—one at the end of each line, whether it makes sense or not! or perhaps he just let the printers have their way in the matter." Salt repunctuated, he implied, to make meaning clearer.[75]

Salt edited *Selected Prose Works of Shelley* (1915) and *Godwin's "Political Justice, A Reprint of the Essay on Property"* (1890). In 1893 he published *Songs of Freedom,* a large selection of English and American poems "illustrative of the growth of the revolutionary ideal—national, social, and intellectual." He included selections from Burns, Southey, Coleridge, Wordsworth, Byron, Shelley, Keats, Whitman, and many others. He believed Whitman to be the successor of Shelley, and he called these two writers the greatest revolutionary poets of the nineteenth century. He included many little-known poets in the anthology, among them Francis Adams and John Barlas. He edited Adams's *Songs of the Army of the*

Night and *The Mass of Christ* (1910) and selections from the *Poems of John E. Barlas* (1925). For many years Salt attempted to revive interest in these two revolutionary poets; but his efforts were to no avail, largely, he felt, because the socialist movement cared little for poets and dreamers.

In 1901 Salt edited *Kith and Kin: Poems of Animal Life*. He admitted that most poetry about animals was third-rate, for poets were often sentimental, unknowing, and unfeeling about animals. Salt contended in the preface that the poets who pioneered in humane presentation of animals were Cowper, Burns, Blake, Coleridge, and Shelley, but he included many poets in the anthology. W. H. Hudson wrote, in a private letter, this trenchant observation about the collection:

I like your anthology and the preface to it. It was not an easy task, and I daresay that you made a wry face over some of the verse that had to be included. If I had to make a collection on your lines, and could afford to publish it myself, and cared not for the public, I should throw over all the detached passages, the gems and quotations from Cowper and others, and give only complete poems. That you could not do; you were bound to be somewhat unjust to your authors. . . . Apropos of your remarks about the better knowledge and feeling of modern times, with regard to our poor relations, resulting in a better poetry, it is curious to find one of the gems of the collection in that very old poem by Andrew Marvell (*The Nymph complaining for the Death of her Fawn*). . . . I am glad you had the courage to include the 'Tiger, tiger, burning bright', the best animal poem in the language. Your morbid friends will probably quarrel with you for that.[76]

The praise of a preeminent naturalist seems completely justified.

The Autobiographies

As autobiographer Salt was most successful in *Seventy Years Among Savages* (1921), which has been used extensively in this study. In *Seventy Years Among Savages,* Salt made advantageous use of his particular perspective on what he called the essential savagery of his fellow islanders. It was questions about dietary practices, in particular the eating of flesh, that first led him to question the values of his civilization. His approach was low-keyed and couched in good humor: "What I write is just a friendly account of friendly savages (by one of them); and I would emphasize the fact that the kindliness and good nature of my fellow-countrymen are in one direction quite as marked features of their character as their savagery is in another. In their own families, to their own kith and kin, to their personal friends—to all those whom fortune has placed within, instead of without the charmed circle of relationship—their conduct . . . is exemplary; it is only where custom or prejudice has dug a gulf of division between their fellow-creatures and themselves that they indulge in the barbarous practices to which I refer."[77]

In the volume, he detailed his own conversion to the new beliefs and causes he had adopted. It is a gracefully written, informative picture of a long-ago Eton, of various romantic socialist movements, of the many humanitarian causes for which Salt worked. He had a large circle of literary friends, and he comments on them as they touched his own life and work, but he never gives the impression of name-dropping. In fact, he is perhaps overly cautious in not capitalizing on such friendships as those with Shaw, Carpenter, and other prominent figures. The book is a charming, accurate reflection of Salt's world from 1851 to 1921.

He ends the written account of his life on a sombre note, as he reflects on the damage to the humanitarian cause inflicted by World War I; yet he was able to maintain a personal optimism, for, like Shelley, he saw in the future a different world, one in which there was a sense of the universal kinship of all creatures.

Salt found himself "discovered" in 1921, for his book was widely noticed; though he complained it was often the anecdotes, and not the message, which claimed attention. One of the most favorable notices appeared in the London *Daily Herald;* Henry W. Nevinson began his review:

For thirty years past I have, with distant admiration, watched Henry Salt moving along his chosen course of beneficent protest against this brutish world—unhastening, unresting. I have counted him among the noble and devoted spirits who, by deeds as well as words, have attempted to redeem the inert and torpid masses around them from our deeply-engrained savagery. I still cannot decide for which of his unpopular causes I admire him most—for his denunciations of flesh-eating, of "blood-sports," of vivisection, of furs and feathers in dress, of the use of pit ponies, of flogging, of prison treatment, of war, of the desecration of mountains for "profit." And my admiration may seem the more remarkable because he would probably reckon me among the "savages" with whom he has spent his seventy years.

Nevinson concluded his review with this remark: ". . . I know that only through the gradual influence of poets of life such as Salt and similar cranks can we ever hope to escape from the barbarism often spoken of as our civilization."[78]

Company I Have Kept (1930) lacks the strong personal point of view of the earlier autobiography, but it does provide many additional details about Salt's friendships, details which were generally not used in *Seventy Years Among Savages.* His reminiscences provide more of the fine points of Salt's life and times and a fuller understanding of the many movements and people he observed. The volume had good notices, including a positive review in the *Times Literary Supplement,* but Salt wrote Joseph Ishill that though the notices were favorable, the book was not selling: "The public want something of a more exciting order—and get it."[79]

The Story of My Cousins (1923) is a gentle book about several animals which shared the lives of the Salts. The animals' biographies give glimpses into the domestic life of the Salts and into the Salts' own sympathetic concern for cats, dogs, and a rook. The accounts show how deeply Salt believed in the Universal Kinship of men and animals; he was convinced that the capacity of animals for friendship and love was not different in kind, only in degree—and not always even in that—from human friendship and love. More than anything else, the quiet stories show that Salt, in his sympathetic understanding for his animal cousins, was one reformer who practiced what he preached. The book was dedicated to Howard Moore, the Chicago teacher whose *The Universal Kinship* was particularly appealing to Salt.

Recollections of Eton

Salt's two accounts of Eton—*Eton under Hornby* (1910), signed O.E., and *Memories of Bygone Eton* (1928), published under his own name, are valuable because of their intimate history of the college and because of their picture of one part of privileged Victorian society between 1866 and 1885. Salt attempted to recall Eton as it was, and not as it appeared to him from the socialist-humanitarian position which he had later adopted. The books project a feeling of honesty throughout. The fuller account in the latter book, incorporating portions of *Eton under Hornby,* contains the serene reflections of an old and wise man who had seen much of his society. Though he condemned much of the privilege that had been his as Eton boy and master, he was able to write about this earlier life with warmth and understanding, and without bitterness. There are amusing memoirs of his father-in-law, the Rev. J. L. Joynes, Sr., who had been Swinburne's tutor, and of J. L. Joynes, Jr., as well as recollections of assorted administrative officials, masters, and students.

Poetry

Salt published a vast quantity of his own poetry in socialist, rationalist, and humanitarian journals. He had a liking for terse expression, and had won a medal at Cambridge for a Greek epigram, which he later published in English:

TWO BETTER THAN ONE

I knew a learn'd Astronomer, who fell,
While stars he studied, in a sunken well.
Saved thence, the wise old man, more cautious grown,
Seeing that Two keep better watch than One,
Vowed that no longer at the skies he'd stare
Alone, but have a boy his walks to share:
And now all's right; for safely both they go,
He heavenward gazing, and the boy below.[80]

As he began publishing poetry for the various causes which captured his attention, Salt's aim was admittedly propagandistic; his poetry, he said in *Cum Grano,* was a weapon which "may not be without its use in the battle against Unreason."[81] He had considerable skill as a "light-armed" versifier, and he clearly believed that it was useful to turn a rhyme and overturn a fool. Several examples of his verse have been quoted in earlier chapters, but this poem from the satiric collection *Homo Rapiens* on a quite different subject deserves reprinting:

TO METCHNIKOFF, THE CIVILIZER

"That splendid chapter of modern physiology and medicine, which is more worth inaugurating a new chronological era than the coming of Christ was."—Joseph McCabe.

"His inoculation of anthropoid apes with syphilis was successful."—*Life of Elie Metchnikoff.*

> Hail, Metchnikoff, great master-mind,
>   Whose thought the future shapes!
> Thou first did'st civilize mankind
>   By syphilizing apes.[82]

Salt's poetry, at least in his later years, generally had good notices. The *TLS* reviewer of *Homo Rapiens* said, ". . . Mr. Salt's humour is the best proof that he is really humane, that he is not, in fact, a superior person exploiting from the standpoint of a barren sanity the brutal stupidity of mankind. It is a stinging humour which pierces every mask of self-interest and predatory hypocrisy, but generally it rises above personal bitterness and it is verbally very accomplished."[83]

Salt was also adept at composing graceful occasional poems, as this tribute to Shaw demonstrates:

ON BERNARD SHAW'S SEVENTIETH BIRTHDAY

(July 1926)

> Speak of Methuselah no more:
>   'Tis "Back to G.B.S."
> What shall the Future praise him for?
>   The fun? the seriousness?

> The illuming thought? the scene on scene
> Portrayed by master mind?
> All these: but most that wit so keen
> Could flash from heart so kind.[84]

As Salt pointed out concerning his work as a translator, he did not consider himself a poet. He did use his verbal and technical skills to point out the folly he saw around him—and to celebrate his friends—but he was under no illusion that he was a Milton or a Shelley.

Salt was a man of letters who wrote on subjects which interested him and which reflected his own philosophic beliefs. Though he had few readers, he believed in himself and what he had to say. In many instances, he had to subsidize his books, as he did with *Literary Sketches* (1888), *The Story of Dido and Aeneas* (1926), *The Story of Aeneas* (1928) (though Shaw's money was used for this subvention), and probably several other of his works. In 1930, he wrote Joseph Ishill that he had come under suspicion from the income tax office because he had little or no income to report from his many books. It was with difficulty, he reported, "that I made the office see that there are some writers who do not write for money!"[85]

Salt was acutely aware that he had no literary following; he was not a good risk for publishers because his books did not make money. He wrote Samuel A. Jones in 1895 that he had ruined one after another publisher with his books on Thoreau.[85] When he was 79, he wrote Joseph Ishill: "My thirty years' work with the Humanitarian League had this effect, among others, that it alienated me from the literary class. I have written books because I *liked* doing so, not because they brought me any profit."[87]

NOTES

1. Henry S. Salt, *Company I Have Kept* (London: George Allen & Unwin, 1930), p. 42.

2. *Ibid.,* p. 51.

3. Henry S. Salt, *Seventy Years Among Savages* (London: George Allen & Unwin, 1921), p. 92.

4. Henry S. Salt, *Percy Bysshe Shelley: A Monograph* (London: Swan Sonnenschein, Lowrey, 1888), p. 225.

5. *Ibid.,* p. 228.

6. Salt, *Seventy Years Among Savages,* p. 93.

7. Salt to Samuel A. Jones, Jones Collection.

8. Henry S. Salt, *Percy Bysshe Shelley: Poet and Pioneer* (London: George Allen & Unwin, 1924), pp. vi–vii.

9. *Ibid.,* p. 5.

10. *Ibid.,* p. 105.

11. Salt, *Seventy Years Among Savages,* pp. 94–95.

12. Archibald Henderson, *George Bernard Shaw: Man of the Century* (New York: Appleton-Century-Crofts, 1965), p. 216.

13. Salt, *Seventy Years Among Savages,* p. 95.

14. *Ibid.,* p. 90.

15. *Ibid.,* p. 98.

16. *Ibid.*

17. Salt to Joseph Ishill, Dec. 30, 1933, in *A Group of Unpublished Letters by Henry S. Salt to Joseph Ishill* (Berkeley Heights, N.J.: Oriole Press, 1942), p. 47; John Davies to John F. Pontin, Nov. 26, 1969: Pontin/Salt collection. All letters from the Pontin/Salt collection cited in this book are published with permission.

18. William David Schaefer, *James Thomson (B.V.): Beyond "The City"* (Berkeley and Los Angeles: University of California Press, 1965), pp. 16–19, 31–36.

19. Salt, *Seventy Years Among Savages,* pp. 103–4.

20. George Hendrick, "Literary Comments in the Letters of Henry S. Salt to W. S. Kennedy," *Emerson Society Quarterly,* No. 19 (II Quarter, 1960), p. 26.

21. Salt to Daniel Ricketson, Nov. 18, 1889, in *Daniel Ricketson and His Friends,* ed. Anna and Walton Ricketson (Boston, Mass.: Houghton, Mifflin, 1904), pp. 249–50.

22. *Ibid.,* p. 251. Salt wrote a similar but briefer letter on Nov. 19, 1889, to T. W. Higginson, requesting information about Higginson's

essay on Thoreau, which Salt had not been able to find. The British Museum Reading Room did not have a copy of Higginson's *Short Studies of American Writers,* where the essay appeared. The letter is in the Houghton Library.

23. H. S. Salt, *The Life of Henry David Thoreau* (London: R. Bentley & Son, 1890), p. v.

24. Salt to T. W. Higginson, Dec. 22, 1889, Houghton Library, Harvard University, published with permission.

25. Quoted in John T. Flanagan, "Henry Salt and His Life of Thoreau," *New England Quarterly,* XXVIII (June, 1955), 238–39. The letters to Bentley are in the University of Illinois Library. Thoreau's efforts to find the Cholmondeley letters failed; they were later edited by Sanborn.

26. *Ibid.,* pp. 239–46.

27. "Thoreau's Life," *The Spectator,* 65 (Oct. 18, 1890), 526–27. The review is unsigned but was probably written by Dr. Japp.

28. Edward Carpenter to Kate Salt, Nov. 5, 1890, Carpenter Collection; Jones to H. G. O. Blake, Aug. 9, 1891, Jones Collection.

29. Salt gave the collection to Professor Raymond Adams; see *Company I Have Kept,* pp. 103–4. I was not allowed to examine the collection.

30. *The Journals of George Sturt* (Cambridge, Eng.: Cambridge University Press, 1967), I, 63, 81.

31. *Daniel Ricketson and His Friends,* pp. 258–59.

32. Salt, *Life of Henry David Thoreau,* 1896 ed., pp. 198, 199.

33. Salt to S. A. Jones, June 9, 1892, Jones Collection; Flanagan, "Henry Salt and His Life of Thoreau," p. 246.

34. John Davies, "Henry S. Salt: A Personal Recollection," *Thoreau Society Bulletin,* No. 29, p. 2. The text of this letter is in the added "Editor's Note."

35. Hendrick, "Literary Comments in the Letters of Henry S. Salt to W. S. Kennedy," p. 28. For his revisions, Salt did have the journals, for Houghton Mifflin had presented him with a set of the Walden edition (20 volumes). These books became the property of John Davies after Salt's death. They later found their way back to the United States, but through the good offices of Leonard Kleinfeld they were returned to Davies. Davies presented the set to John Pontin. The letter to Jones is in the Jones Collection.

36. Howard Williams, *The Ethics of Diet* (London: Swan Sonnenschein, 1896), pp. 520–23. For Gandhi's comment see Gandhi's *Auto-*

biography: The Story of My Experiments with Truth (Washington, D.C.: Public Affairs Press, 1948), p. 68.

37. Gandhi, *Autobiography,* p. 67.

38. Pyarelal [Nair], *Mahatma Gandhi: The Early Phase* (Ahmedabad: Navajivan, 1965), I, 264–65.

39. Salt to Gandhi, Sept. 18, 1929, Gandhi National Museum and Library, New Delhi.

40. Gandhi to Salt, Oct. 12, 1929. I have followed the punctuation in *Company I Have Kept,* pp. 100–101. The carbon in the Gandhi National Museum and Library, New Delhi, is not corrected, as the original undoubtedly was.

41. See my dissertation, "Thoreau and Gandhi: A Study of the Development of 'Civil Disobedience' and Satyagraha," University of Texas, 1954.

42. Salt, *Seventy Years Among Savages,* p. 62.

43. The essay is reprinted in Salt's *Literary Sketches* (London: Swan Sonnenschein, Lowrey, 1888), see pp. 51–52.

44. *Ibid.,* p. 55.

45. H. S. Salt, *Tennyson as a Thinker* (London: William Reeves, 1893), p. 9.

46. *Ibid.,* p. 20.

47. *Ibid.,* p. 56.

48. Salt, *Company I Have Kept,* p. 183.

49. Shaw to Pakenham Beatty, April 4, 1893, in Bernard Shaw, *Collected Letters 1874–1897* (London: Max Reinhardt, 1965), p. 388.

50. Henry S. Salt, *De Quincey* (London: George Bell & Sons, 1904), p. 10.

51. Henry S. Salt, *Richard Jefferies: His Life & His Ideals* (London: Arthur C. Fifield, 1905), pp. 38, 68.

52. Salt, *Company I Have Kept,* pp. 105–6. Salt sent Samuel Jones a copy of Besant's remarkable letter.

53. *Ibid.,* p. 106.

54. Henry S. Salt, *On Cambrian and Cumbrian Hills* (London: A. C. Fifield, 1908, rev. 1922), p. 25.

55. *Ibid.,* p. 112.

56. Henry S. Salt, *The Call of the Wildflower* (London: George Allen & Unwin, 1922), p. 9.

57. *Ibid.,* p. 10.

58. *Ibid.,* p. 133.

59. Salt, *Company I Have Kept,* p. 200.

60. Henry S. Salt, *Treasures of Lucretius* (London: Watts, 1912), p. 10.

61. *Ibid.,* p. 11.

62. *Ibid.,* p. 45.

63. Shaw to Salt, Sept. 14, 1926, University of Texas and Berg Collection. The postmark is slightly blurred, and the typescript at the University of Texas is dated "14th Sept. (?) 1926. The original is in the Berg Collection.

64. Shaw to Salt, Oct. 3, 1926, University of Texas and Berg Collection. The original is in the Berg Collection.

65. Shaw to Salt, Jan. 13, 1928, University of Texas and Berg Collection. The original is in the Berg Collection.

66. Salt, *Company I Have Kept,* p. 202.

67. *Ibid.,* p. 203.

68. Salt to Shaw, Feb. 7, 1928, British Library.

69. *TLS,* Jan. 24, 1929, p. 55.

70. Salt to Joseph Ishill, April, 1930, in *A Group of Unpublished Letters by Henry Salt to Joseph Ishill,* pp. 11–12.

71. Hendrick, "Literary Comments in the Letters of Henry S. Salt to W. S. Kennedy," p. 28.

72. H. D. Thoreau, *Anti-Slavery and Reform Papers,* ed. Henry S. Salt (London: Swan Sonnenschein, 1890), p. 9.

73. Salt to Jones, March 8, 15, 1894, Jones Collection.

74. Salt to Jones, Dec. 2, 1895, Jones Collection.

75. Salt to Jones, Jan. 4, 1896, Jones Collection.

76. Salt, *Company I Have Kept,* p. 123.

77. Salt, *Seventy Years Among Savages,* pp. 9–10.

78. Reprinted in *Cum Grano: Verses and Epigrams* (Berkeley Heights, N.J.: Oriole Press, 1931), pp. vii–x.

79. *TLS,* Aug. 7, 1930; *A Group of Unpublished Letters by Henry Salt to Joseph Ishill,* p. 19.

80. Salt, *Cum Grano,* p 113.

81. *Ibid.,* p. vii.

82. Henry S. Salt, *Homo Rapiens* (London: Watts & Co., 1926), p. 14.

83. *TLS,* Dec. 23, 1926, p. 951.

84. Salt, *Cum Grano,* p. 89.

85. *A Group of Unpublished Letters by Henry Salt to Joseph Ishill,* p. 16.

86. Salt to Jones, Oct. 16, 1895, Jones Collection.

87. *A Group of Unpublished Letters by Henry Salt to Joseph Ishill,* p. 13.

CHAPTER

5

Salt and His Friends

From all accounts, Henry Salt was a quiet, unassuming man, reticent about his own accomplishments, acutely aware of human foibles and savagery, yet believing as Shelley and Thoreau did in the possibility of a better world. He knew most of the English socialists during the early 1880s and through the 1890s, and he was devoted to his friends but not blind to their follies. He resigned from the Fabian Society in 1901, in protest against Fabian support of the Boer War, but he did not break his ties with his old socialist and Fabian friends; he knew that the socialists could not agree among themselves, and he seemingly did not wish to increase the discord with bitter statements attacking those who supported the war. Though he stopped his most active socialist work, as he devoted increasing amounts of time to the Humanitarian League, he remained a committed socialist throughout his life.

In his autobiographies, Salt told amusing and pertinent stories about many of his socialist friends, but in most cases it is clear that his relationships with them were not on intimate personal terms. Such was not the case, however, with two of the most prominent socialists: Shaw, a Fabian, and Carpenter, an Ethical Socialist. A good deal of their correspondence and other first-hand material has survived, and it is possible to reconstruct a part of the unusual complicated relationships between the Shaws, the Salts, and Carpenter. In 1905, when Shaw's memory was better than it was in 1950 when he wrote the preface to *Salt and His Circle,* he wrote Archibald Henderson, his appointed biographer, an account of his relationship with the Salts:

I joined the Land Reform Union, and met there James Leigh Joynes, an Eton master (son of a well known Eton dignitary), Sydney Olivier, and Henry Hyde Champion, besides two Christian Socialist clergymen, Steward Headlam and Symes of Nottingham. . . .

   Now Joynes was a vegetarian, a humanitarian, a Shelleyan. He had just been deprived of his Eton post because he had made a tour in Ireland with [Henry] George. . . . Joynes's sister was married to another Eton master, Henry Salt. Salt was also a vegetarian, a humanitarian, a Shelleyan, a De Quinceyite. He loathed Eton, being a born revolutionist. As soon as he had saved enough to live with a Thoreau-like simplicity in a laborer's cottage in the country (he had no children) he threw up his post and shook the dust of Eton off his feet. Instead of working at Socialism, he founded the Humanitarian League, of which he is still secretary. He and I and his wife, Kate Salt, with whom I used to play endless pianoforte duets on the noisiest grand piano that ever descended from Eton to a Surrey cottage, became very close friends. My article "A Sunday on the Surrey Hills" . . . describes my first visit to them in [the] country (I had visited them once before at Eton with Joynes), and several scenes of my Pleasant & Unpleasant plays were written in the heather on Limpsfield Common during my visits to them at Oxted (they did not stay very long at Tilford, the scene of the article). Here you have the link between me and the Humanitarians. Another intimate of the Salt household was Edward Carpenter, the author of Towards Democracy, whose works give you the man. We called him the Noble Savage. We also played duets; and we all wore sandals (in the house—though Carpenter used them out of doors too) which he had taught a workman friend of his to make at Millthorpe, a village near Sheffield at which he resided. In this circle there was no question of Henry George and Karl Marx, but a good deal of Walt Whitman & Thoreau. The worst that happened was the death of Joynes, who was slaughtered by a medical treatment so grossly and openly stupid & ruinous that I have never forgiven the medical profession for it since.[1]

In this carefully worded section, though Shaw is providing information to his biographer about his close friendship and intellectual ties with the Salts and Joynes, he does not explore the significance of the relationships. Nor does he mention the "Sunday husband" arrangement with Kate. The death of Joynes had a lasting impact on both the Salts and Shaw. According to Shaw, the doctors ordered whiskey for Joynes, who was suffering from what Shaw thought was a trifling heart complaint; they immobilized him and caused him to die of an enlarged liver. The Salts hid their deepest emotions concerning Joynes's death, but Shaw gave full vent to his outrage in his slashing denunciation of doctors in the preface to *The Doctor's Dilemma*.

Kate Salt, intellectual and emotional, was important to Shaw and Carpenter in quite different ways. The two men had an intellectual and musical companion without any of the usual rights or responsibilities of marriage. Kate Salt's first correspondence in 1886 with Carpenter was slightly formal; the letters were those of a well-read late-Victorian lady converted to socialism. By the 1890s, however, she was writing Edward Carpenter passionate letters of idealized love.

Edward wrote Kate in 1890 from Ceylon about Hinduism and Thoreau's use of the *Bhagavad-Gita:*

I am glad you are helping Mrs. B.[esant] at the Girls' Club. She is such a good woman, and I think you will like the work among the girls. I think the Theosophists are doing some good work—although as far as I can make out their teaching is of a somewhat secondhand character. One of my objects in coming out here has been to study the ancient occult or divine knowledge with my friend Armáchalam—as it has been handed down for really unnumbered centuries in this part of the world. . . .

There is no doubt that they have a tradition—corroborated by ever new experience—of facts about birth & death, the soul's union with God, its powers, destiny, &c wh. throws all our Western religions into the shade—and which facts are only most dimly realised, if at all by people in our regions. Of course it interests me tremendously to find that these facts corroborate the ideas indicated in T. D. [*Towards Democracy*] most closely. I had thought before that it w^d be so—but could not feel certain till now. The most intimate & esoteric teaching here is thoroughly democratic. While preserving the belief in Caste as a veil for the lower stages it ultimately lays it aside completely—and such words as Freedom, Equality, Joy become its watchwords. The individual "I" ascends & becomes one with the universal "I", & sharer of the most intense happiness, without at the same time losing its true individuality. And this is an actual experience realised here to-day & recorded from the very earliest date of human history on earth at least 10,000 years ago in identical terms. I have no doubt that Thoreau knew something about this, and that was why he read the Indian works so assiduously (but they want reading between the lines). That last page or so of Walden exactly expresses what out here is known to be an everyday fact. The beautiful bug does come out at last! I am inclined to think that the time has come when the Western nations will come into the inheritance of this great tradition which has been preserved so many centuries here—and which even now is only fully understood by a few in this country or India. I hope you have read the Bhagvat Gita by this time. Read it quietly

& attentively & don't believe what any notes say upon it! & I think you will find much in it—tho' it only deals with a portion of the subject in question.[2]

In Kate's response to this calm, literary letter, her feelings and emotions tumbled out to "T.D.," as she addressed him:

Thanks for the beautiful letter (dated Nov. 24) which came in last night (the postman had been 6 times already!) just as I was putting away my sandal work—at the end of a most depressing day of thick, heavy, remorseless fog—a fog that was slowly but surely squeezing one's soul into a corner to make room for a big black fiend of pessimism & despair! Do you know that feeling? when one struggles in vain—although one *knows* that all the time the sky is there behind and that the fog must pass—Dear T. D.! and then in came your letter, talking so calmly & confidently of those things that I most long to believe,—to believe *reasonably,* that is; for I do believe now—only unreasonably;—I can't tell you what a "God-send" it was to me.—Why do you say *"write letters"*! Don't you know that I can't write sense, and that if I indulged in letter-writing to you you would soon be irritated beyond endurance. I'm too self-conscious to be able to write comfortably to any one; so I choose postcards as the safest & most respectable method.—If I could succeed in entirely merging *E. C.* in *T. D.* in my imagination, it would be easy enough to write!—but there's always that tiresome old E. C. to be considered;—what will he think? will he be cross? will he think me too familiar, or intruding? shall I bore him?—or madden him! Perhaps he'll snap. . . . No; I've not finished reading the Bhagavad Gita yet;—have read 12 chapters. Am relieved by your warning about the notes! . . . It is all quite new to me—and yet at the same time infinitely old. I have a strange sensation as I read that there are things which I have always known; I am reminded of a light from a window—a certain feeling that instantly carries me back, as one might be swept back through a tunnel—but this is a thing that I've never been able to explain to anyone—so don't attend to it! and don't think me wandering.— One can feel how beautiful the writing must be in the original.—I find it wonderfully helpful; & intensely interesting; I can't tell you *how* much so.—There is a strong thread of T. D. (*not* E. C.! but T. D.) running all through it. Had you read it when you wrote *T. D.?*—however it makes no difference,—it was no *book* that taught you what you know.—You funny Chips; you say "You have been *so good* about *T. D.!*" Don't you know, then, what I really think of it? To use a mere phrase, I think it is the most important book of our time; but no words could say for me how, personally, I love and worship it, and find in it my highest creed and hope and ideal—all that I have dumbly & feebly felt after—all that I have come close to in the best moments of my life. And to find it all expressed! written down! It is as though you had caught the very clouds; seized on the very winds;—but it's no use my trying to talk about *T. D.*—it is too far beyond all words. . . . I like to think of that shawl going with you in your evening walks.—I really had no *choice* about sending it. A silent force compelled me that day; I've often marvelled about it since.—And I was afraid it might annoy you! Perhaps some of my unuttered love & reverence for *T. D.* may be clinging about its "folds", and helping to keep you warm.[3]

This letter gives an indication of what Kate Salt's conversations must have been like and furnishes clues as to why she was admired by both Bernard Shaw and Edward Carpenter. By 1890, Carpenter was a cult figure, because of his *Towards Democracy* and because of his almost open homosexual life. Kate gave him a glimpse into the emotional life of a woman, but she was not a sexual threat to him.

Shaw had a lesser reputation than Carpenter during the first years of the friendship, but Kate Salt was apparently important to him because of the easy conversation in the Salt household, the music, and the relaxing atmosphere. Henry Salt and Jim Joynes were his intellectual companions, sharing the same basic ideas. Shaw, we can speculate, knowing of Kate's lesbianism, was relieved of the urge to philander. In 1950, Shaw wrote, "I was always happy at the Salts. We never talked politics but gossiped endlessly about our friends and everything else."[4] It is probably untrue that they "never talked politics."

During the early years of their friendship, Shaw wrote in the preface to *Salt and His Circle,* Shaw and Carpenter were (nonsexual) "Sunday husbands" of Kate. That particular kind of relationship (with and without sexual overtones) apparently fascinated Shaw. In *Getting Married* (1908) he quoted Shakespeare as saying "that a woman wanted a Sunday husband as well as a weekday one." And in *The Millionairess* (1935) there is a discussion of both Sunday husbands and wives, and the comments are obviously sexual. There has been speculation that Shaw used Kate and the "Sunday husband" relationship in *Candida.* Archibald Henderson, in the final edition of his biography of Shaw, wrote: "*Candida* was drawn from life. . . . *Candida* was modeled after Kate Salt, a brilliant, fascinating woman. The model for Morell was Edward Carpenter, a Socialist, and for a time an Anglican priest. Shaw was the model for Marchbanks, although he vehemently denied his identity with the poet."[5] Henderson does not give a source for these assertions, but he was undoubtedly following Winsten, who also made such an unsupported statement in *Salt and His Circle.* In the surviving letters to Carpenter, Kate does not comment on whether or not she recognized herself, and Henry did not make such an identification in any of his published statements on Shaw. It is certainly possible that Shaw made use of Kate and the "Sunday husband" arrangement in the formulation of characters and ideas in the play, but there is no supporting evidence. Shaw's art is much more complex than Henderson realized. It is true that Winsten published a previously unknown essay by Henry Salt on Shaw quoting Carpenter as saying, after hearing *Candida* read, "No, Shaw. It won't do."[6] But that does not prove Carpenter was the prototype of Morell, nor Kate of Candida.

Kate could speak sharply and truthfully to Shaw, and her honesty and strength of character are quite like Candida's. Concerning *Arms and the Man,* written just before *Candida,* Kate had this conversation with Shaw, as recorded in Henry's diary and published by Henderson:

Shaw, wildly exuberant over the completion of *Arms and the Man* (1894), defiantly asserted: "Mozart is bigger than Wagner as I am bigger than Ibsen."

"You haven't proved it yet."

"I want to reach the melting point in human beings through laughter. I want the people to go away from my plays feeling a little bigger than when they came to them. To have laughed themselves out of littleness."

"I hope you will. You have it in you but I doubt if you have the courage. It needs a kind of courage . . . a courage you do not possess. You are more likely to run away from the really big effort and find sport in little things. It is so much more amusing. There is something feline [in you] I think. I love cats but I do not think them big when they are playing with a mouse."[7]

Kate's charge that Shaw ran away "from the really big effort" would appear to have been true at times. There are some special reasons for believing Shaw may have chosen not to make use of some of Kate's sexual views which were, she felt, the basis for *You Never Can Tell.*

Kate wrote Edward Carpenter on January 28, 1899, a long confessional letter, only a brief portion of which is reproduced here:

I wanted *so* much to write you a sort of history of myself—to try & clear up any mistakes about my nature!—I felt, after our fragmentary talk that day at Sheffield, and your letter since, that I really must try and write it all; for when, after all, do I ever get a chance of talking quite peacefully and uninterruptedly with you? really *never.* I can't talk if either *I* am just going away, or *you* are just going away, or if we are having a walk with a beginning & an end to it—or if I feel that you are taking precautions all the time to keep me at a proper distance! But I thought on paper I should be able to talk to you just as freely as to my own self.—However I've tried and tried—and my word! it *was* a job. It all looked so artificial & ridiculous—and I kept altering & patching and it only got worse—and after all it is rather stupid that I can't tell you quite simply & straightforwardly (face to face) what I like & what I don't like, and answer any questions my Krishna cares to ask!—I certainly have never consciously "kept you in the dark"!—but I suppose I've been more or less in the dark myself.—This much at least I know, that my instinctive repulsion for any physical intimacy with the other sex could never be altered by any possible experience. I remember telling Shaw once that the shuddering horror felt by him (or any normal man) at the thought of being touched or fondled by one of his own sex, is no stronger than my own feeling with regard to the touch of the opposite sex. (Whereupon doubting Thomas went & wrote a play called 'You Never Can Tell'!)[8]

Was Kate correct in her speculation that she had given Shaw the idea for *You Never Can Tell*? Everything contained in her correspondence with Carpenter indicates she was an honest reporter of events. She may have had (though there is no direct proof) an emotional attachment to Shaw, and indeed her telling him of her sexual preferences before 1895 when Shaw began the play, and long before she told Carpenter, provides a clue as to how openly she must have talked with Shaw. Shaw himself said she loved him as much as she could love any man. Did Shaw tell Kate that he used her idea? He certainly had ample opportunity, for he often called at the Salts' rooms in London for an evening of music with Kate, and for a time before his marriage Kate acted as his unpaid secretary. Shaw's letters to Charlotte Payne-Townshend often mention Kate, sometimes humorously, sometimes in a seeming attempt to provoke Charlotte's jealousy. After Kate began work for Shaw, Charlotte also began doing secretarial work for him. Kate was apparently distressed at having a rival and went to Shaw to inquire about the secretaryship. Quite accustomed to such triangles, for he had participated in them several times previously, Shaw made the most of it, though he said he was cross and "put out." In writing to Charlotte of his session with Kate he said he began dictating to Kate as if he "had never dictated to anybody else." Then he added cryptically: "In the absence of sentimental interruptions we get along famously. . . ."[9] The ambiguity was probably planned, and his intent was undoubtedly to make the rich Charlotte Payne-Townshend jealous. There is no indication that Kate, distressed by Shaw's marriage, gave herself a place of importance in the genesis of *You Never Can Tell*. Shaw began the play before he met Payne-Townshend, and he gives us one internal clue which would confirm Kate's theory. In Act II, Valentine, a character with many of Shaw's own quirks and views, is seated at the table next to Gloria, a character with many of Kate's views; Valentine looks around for something and William, the comic waiter, says to him, "Salt at your elbow, sir." It is reasonable to assume that the line was intended for Kate's amusement.

Shaw often insisted that *You Never Can Tell* was a "potboiler," and one of his reasons for thinking so may have been his inability, because of censorship, to deal in a forthright way with the theme suggested by Kate. During the writing of the play he met Payne-Townshend, and it appears that he used the play as part of his campaign to marry her. There were some similarities between Kate and Charlotte, for while Charlotte may not have been as opposed to the touch of a man as Kate was, she seems to have had no intention of entering into a physical relationship, and there are strong hints that Shaw's own marriage was not consummated.[10] Shaw may have thought—assuming that he knew Charlotte's attitudes on sex and physical contact in 1896—that he could dissuade her from her views. St. John Irvine says that Shaw as an old man was sorry that he had not been more insistent with Charlotte in sexual matters.[11] Both Kate and Charlotte were socialists and both were rebels. In the writing of the play, Shaw may have used an idea from Kate, dramatized it in a socially acceptable way, hoping the play would be a commercial success, and he may have added sections which would appeal to Charlotte, hoping it would help him win his millionairess. But the farce is not the "really big effort" to which Kate said she had challenged Shaw.

Gloria in the play has many of Kate's qualities; she is described as "high-minded" and "inexperienced." She had been specially trained by her high-minded mother to carry on women's rights work. Shaw presents part of himself in Valentine—failure, trifler with the hearts of women—and the importance of touch in the play at first centers around Valentine, the dental surgeon, whose touch is painful if an extra five shillings is not paid for gas. When the play begins, young Dolly has just had a tooth extracted, without gas. Although Valentine had brought pain to the girl, she accepted it because it was his business "to hurt people." She was fascinated by him, and she asked him dozens of questions and brought him into her family circle. The first act ends with a gruesome scene involving Valentine's professional touching of a person of his own sex—Mr. Crampton, his landlord, who had "taken a fancy" to the dentist. Crampton had a broken tooth but did not want gas, for he had been taught to bear pain. After Crampton was in the chair, Valentine let down the back of the chair, placing Crampton in a helpless position. Valentine then put the gas mouthpiece over Crampton's face. The act ends with this description which might be interpreted as a scene of homosexual rape: *"He presses the mouthpiece over Crampton's mouth and nose, leaning over his chest so as to hold his head and shoulders well down on the chair. Crampton makes an inarticulate sound in the mouthpiece and tries to lay hands on Valentine, whom he supposes to be in front of him. After a moment his arms wave aimlessly, then subside and drop. He is quite insensible. Valentine throws aside the mouthpiece quickly; picks the forceps adroitly from the glass; and—"*[12]

Shaw presents one other scene involving the touch of men, and it, too, was acceptable on the stage. After the luncheon in the hotel, Valentine, in ecstasy over his love for Gloria, rushes away, bounding into William. The two men save each other from falling *"by clutching one another tightly around the waist and whirling one another round."* William declares the whole event, "Very natural, sir, I'm sure, sir, at your age,"[13] and Valentine gives William his earnings for the past six months—Dolly's crown piece.

Touch plays an important part throughout the play. When Mrs. Clandon and M'Comas meet, their handshake *"is that of old friends after a long separation."* In the battle of the sexes between Valentine and Gloria in Act II, when Valentine is beginning to win the battle, he declares his love. The stage directions then are as follows: *"He turns towards her as if the impulse to touch her were ungovernable: she rises and stands on her guard wrathfully. He springs up impatiently and retreats a step."*[14] Moved by Valentine's passionate speech, Gloria warns Valentine not to go on telling her what he feels; she has, by this time, had her resistance broken. Valentine seizes Gloria's hands, as she looks at him in terror, and kisses her, declaring they are in love. According to the stage directions, she could *"only gasp at him."*[15] Valentine, being called by the twins, kisses Gloria's hands and rushes away.

The next touch in the play is between two women: Gloria and her mother. Gloria, greatly puzzled by the chemical attraction to Valentine, wants to but cannot talk to her mother. According to the stage directions, Gloria *"suddenly throws her arm about her mother and embraces her almost passionately."* Mrs. Clandon is "embarrassed" and declares that Gloria is becoming "sentimental."[16] Mrs. Clandon, we learn in the play, has never been in love, and she is incapable of helping her daughter.

At the end of the last act, Valentine admits he has been amused at breaking down Gloria's advanced ideas, but he declares he was attempting to break down her heart, and in doing so, it was he who was transported. Gloria confesses her shame at the feeling of losing control over herself, blushes, and covers her face with her left hand, supporting herself by putting her right hand on his arm. Valentine declares he is losing his senses again, and Gloria takes her hand from her face, puts it on his right shoulder, and looks him in the eyes. Valentine declares his poverty; she says he could earn money: "Valentine [*half delighted, half frightened*]. I never could: you'd be unhappy. My dearest love: I should be the merest fortune-hunting adventurer if—[*Her grip of his arms tightens; and she kisses him.*] Oh Lord!"[17] Shaw was indeed the doubting Thomas, as he has his heroine touch and kiss the hero; Kate could not have done so. It is also reasonable to assume that Shaw was writing directly to Charlotte the heiress; Valentine is perplexed and nervous, but the philosophic waiter assures Valentine that marriage turns out to be comfortable, enjoyable, and happy, "some of the time." William says his own wife is like Gloria: "commanding" and with a "masterful disposition," but the waiter would do it again.[18]

If Kate was correct when she told Carpenter that she gave Shaw the idea for the play, the continued emphasis on touch in the play takes on new meaning, showing how Shaw made touch between man and man and woman and woman acceptable; but Shaw did not have the courage to explore the subject proposed by Kate.

Kate did not go out of Shaw's thoughts after his marriage. On August 2, 1903, he wrote Salt that a review copy of *Man and Superman* was being sent "so that Kate can read it and you review it (if you like). . . . The book is one of the most colossal efforts of the human mind, and contains several passages which you will find congenial, and which will make Kate blush for having gradually argued herself into a conviction that I am a lost soul."[19]

Why did Kate think Shaw a lost soul? The evidence is not clear, and most of the letters she wrote Carpenter at this time were destroyed. Was it because she felt Shaw took the easy way out in his search for commercial success, that he shied away from the "big effort"? Was it because of Shaw's marriage to Charlotte Payne-Townshend? Henry Salt was a witness to the marriage. Was Salt there because he was a friend, or did Shaw invite him to hurt Kate? The reason or reasons now seem beyond recovery.

Shaw's marriage, however, did affect the Salts, for after the ceremony the Salts and Shaw were never again intimate friends as they had been previously. Shaw wrote a comic account of his wedding, an account in which Salt is prominently mentioned:

I was very ill when I was married, altogether a wreck on crutches and in an old jacket which the crutches had worn to rags. I had asked my friends, Mr. Graham Wallas, of the London School Board, and Mr. Henry Salt, the biographer of Shelley and De Quincey, to act as witnesses, and, of course, in honour of the occasion they were dressed in their best clothes. The registrar never imagined I could possibly be the bridegroom; he took me for the inevitable beggar who completes all wedding processions.[20]

Shaw also wrote this account for *The Star:*

As a lady and gentleman were out driving in Henrietta-st., Covent-garden yesterday, a heavy shower drove them to take shelter in the office of the Superintendent Registrar there, and in the confusion of the moment he married them. The lady was an Irish lady named Miss Payne-Townshend, and the gentleman was George Bernard Shaw.

Mr. Graham Wallas and Mr. H. S. Salt were also driven by stress of weather into the registrar's, and the latter being secretary of the Humanitarian League would naturally have remonstrated against the proceedings had there been time, but there wasn't. Mr. Bernard Shaw means to go off to the country next week to recuperate, and this is the second operation he has undergone lately, the first being conducted, not by a registrar, but by a surgeon.

Startling as was the liberty undertaken by the Henrietta-st. official, it turns out well. Miss Payne-Townshend is an Irish lady with an income many times the volume of that which "Corno di Bassetto" used to earn, but to that happy man, being a vegetarian, the circumstance is of no moment. The lady is deeply interested in the London School of Economics, and that is the common ground on which the brilliant couple met. Years of married bliss to them.[21]

Carpenter wrote Kate on June 8, 1898, "I suppose G. B. S. has disappeared from yr. horizon—what a change!"[22] Unfortunately her reply was apparently among those letters destroyed by Carpenter and Salt.

Was the new Mrs. Shaw jealous of Kate, or did Kate herself want to end the friendship? Catherine Mandeville Salt wrote Shaw in 1939 that her husband "always said it was entirely Kate's fault that you ceased to meet as in the old days."[23] Whatever the reasons for the rupture of the friendship, when Kate died in 1919, Shaw wrote Salt a long letter, with these revealing passages:

The loss of one's wife after ten years is only the end of an adventure. After thirty it is the end of an epoch. From that on it becomes more and more the end of everything. Fortunately, over people like us, who never get past their work, and who never would have invented marriage if we had not found it in the world, death has no great power.

Kate's death ends for me an intention that always haunted me, if haunting is the right word for an entirely pleasant obsession. My old visits to Oxted were quite unlike any other experience of the sort, and occupied a place of their own in my life. It was not solely because Kate spoilt me and pampered me most outrageously that I found them so harmonious. There was a congeniality so complete that the word seems ridiculous, as suitable only for states imperfect enough to make one conscious of them. I suppose it was the Shelleyan nexus that bound us.

Well, I never could think of that as a thing of the past. I took it for granted that some day I should escape from my anything but simple life, and spend another fortnight with you in the old way. I never did escape; and now I never shall.[24]

Shaw in his 1950 preface to *Salt and His Circle* wrote that toward the end of Kate's life, he turned up at the Salts' house unexpectedly and that she "flung her arms" around him. Over half a century after *You Never Can Tell* was written, Shaw was having Kate touch him.

The friendship of Salt and Shaw, though not as close as before, was not to end because of Kate's unhappiness with Shaw. Many of Shaw's letters to Salt are now available in the first two volumes of Shaw's *Collected Letters*. There are some comic personal letters and several concerning humanitarian work. Shaw was a willing ally of Salt's in the humanitarian movement, but Salt found that having Shaw's endorsement had its drawbacks, for the famous dramatist was quixotic and often argued causes from eccentric points of view. For instance, in the preface to *Killing for Sport,* edited by Salt, Shaw said, "My own pursuits as a critic and as a castigator of morals by ridicule (otherwise a writer of comedies) are so cruel that in point of giving pain to many worthy people I can hold my own with most dentists, and beat a skillful sportsman hollow.

I know many sportsmen, and none of them are ferocious. I know several humanitarians; and they are all ferocious. No book of sport breathes such a wrathful spirit as this book of humanity. No sportsman wants to kill the fox or the pheasant as I want to kill him when I see him doing it."[25] Shaw's paradoxes could hardly have pleased Salt, and, in fact, Shaw's observations on humanitarians cannot with justice be applied to Salt.

Salt was a tolerant man, and he seems to have seen beyond personal quirks to the essential nature of people; he continued to believe Shaw to be a kindhearted humanitarian. Shaw obviously did not think the preface to *Killing for Sport* was an affront to Salt, and at one time facetiously suggested that he would write a book called *The Real Salt,* but did not ever undertake such a work.

A letter of Salt to Shaw in 1939 helps explain why the two men remained friends. Not long before his death, Salt wrote:

I read varying reports of you in the papers, which leave nothing certain except that in the course of a few years you and I will have to present our credentials in high quarters. . . .

I have had a sickly winter here; and even now cannot regain my footing. I stagger from room to room, clutching at mantel-pieces &c and any projectile which tells me where I am; I never go out of doors; prefer to fall on my own floor—

But do not assume I have no ideals. A few years ago, a girl of nearly my age, to whom I had been much attached, in the twenties, wrote to tell me she had counted my birth-days for sixty years, but thought she would write at last. We met, and had a most agreeable talk, recapitulating and reconsidering past errors & what should I have done whereas in fact I forgot all other obligations and married Kate. I told her I attributed this lapse of conduct to an Irishman whom I knew. We became good friends again, and now correspond.

My wife took the chair at the tea table, as a sort of judge or referee. What do you think of that? Does it not knock your ideals into bits?[26]

Did Salt's memory fail him in thinking that Shaw had been responsible for his marriage to Kate? Or is the story merely for comic effect?

Shaw recognized that his friend was a man of principle, and Shaw's summation of their relationship in the preface to *Salt and His Circle* is not without envy: "My pastime has been writing sermons in plays, sermons preaching what Salt practised."

The Salts' friendship with Carpenter did not end on the same serene note. If Kate did declare her Platonic love for Shaw, those declarations were in person and not in writing; but she declared her affection for Carpenter in letters which have survived. Perhaps the most painful one was written on February 17, 1897:

> I came to see you because—well I don't know why exactly, but I felt I *must* try and make it better—Please dear Only One don't think it very bad of me to bother you. I find there's only YOU in all the world—so you see it *is* rather important for me—Edward! don't leave me altogether if you can help it. I have really tried hard—but it is *so* hard—and sometimes I feel as if I shall go down.—*You know you know* I don't want to torment you—but when I feel I am absolutely nothing to you it seems so impossible to go on.[27]

Carpenter's response to this outburst is missing, presumably destroyed. I have quoted earlier in this chapter Kate's confessional letter in which she talked about her horror at being touched by a man. After that confession, Kate wrote Carpenter several letters mentioning her friend Mary, who had gone to New York. In one, she wrote "dear old Ted" that he was the only one she wanted to talk to about the affair, for nobody else would understand. In one of her most intense letters, she refers to her sexual nature, Carpenter's banishment of her, and her reasons for staying with Henry.[28] The explanatory details are not available, for most of the other letters of this period which might be used to gloss this second letter were apparently destroyed. Most of the letter is too painful to quote, but this brief section, a part of which was quoted in Chapter 1, does help us understand her feelings toward Henry:

We two poor things dwelling here together like friendly strangers—no touch possible (oh! the pity of it!) and no understanding. But 20 years bring deep deep chains that could never be cut through, and I'm really thankful and content, and I want you to know that this is true. It is something not to have added a deeper wrong to the first deep wrong that I did him. But it is dreadful to feel that one has never brought Peace to anyone.—I might have brought it to *her*,—to Mary.—if God had not planted us on either side of a great ocean, granting only one little look into each other's eyes. Edward, Ted, do you know that after that week with her in Yorkshire, when we met Henry and Bess at Windermere, and Mary went across the road to sleep as there was not room for all, I had the most awful moment of *awakening* that I've ever known in my life. I had never before realised *what* I had done in letting myself get married. At the same time, such profound *Pity* took hold of me, seeing as for the first time what I had done to *him* by marrying him, that I believe he was safe from that moment—I mean I could never have thought again of deserting him—poor lonely thing.—O Darkie! Why do I talk to you for ever about myself, when you never never talk to *me*. And will it always be so?

This letter, perhaps the most disturbing one left in the Kate-Carpenter correspondence, gives us valuable insight into her emotional nature, but it raises more questions than it answers about Henry Salt. What did Kate's turmoil do to his own inner life? Did he ignore or accept Kate's sexual attitudes? The evidence on which to base conclusive answers to these questions is missing, as it is for the question whether their frequent moves hampered Henry's work in the humanitarian movement and his writing career. Kate had a restless nature, and the Salts moved from one country cottage to another, from one flat in London to another.

The Salts did, in one of their last moves, build a cottage in 1910 near Carpenter's home at Millthorpe, and they lived there seven years. Winsten reports that both Salts were disillusioned after living in such close proximity to Carpenter; specifically, Winsten suggests that Kate discovered that Carpenter did not understand women. Whatever her disappointment in Carpenter, Kate continued to correspond with him after they left the cottage near Millthorpe, but the letters lacked the intensity of the earlier ones. The causes of Henry's disillusionment were probably many; when he wrote an essay for a volume after Carpenter's death, he praised Carpenter's early writings but indicated that the later ones were overrated. He recorded the accepted view of Carpenter—a philosophic yogi, completely self-possessed—then demolished that image, discussing at length the agitated mind behind *Towards Democracy,* denying that Carpenter had the intellectual power of Whitman. Carpenter's moods were a trial for all of his friends. Henry regarded Carpenter as "a seer, a prophet, rather than a thinker; not always logical in his reasoning, but speaking as if *ex cathedra,* with the authority that his opinions derived from a rare and magnetic personality. He was a mystic, inclined to be a believer in occult powers, though he himself did not possess any. . . . There was certainly something abnormal in him; and the same quality must have been inherent in some of his writings, notably in *Towards Democracy,* which brought pilgrims from every part of the world to his Derbyshire hamlet."[29] Salt's essay is written with great honesty and perception, the work of a friend, but an objective one.

Another socialist friend of the Salts was Sydney Olivier (Lord Olivier). Lady Olivier, in her selection of letters and writings of her husband, dated the friendship from about 1885, the year the Oliviers married. The Oliviers spent one summer holiday at Tilford. Lady Olivier referred to Kate as one of their greatest friends. Henry and Sydney were fellow humanitarians and nature lovers. Though their correspondence is not extensive, the closeness of their friendship is reflected in the letter by Sydney after Kate's death:

Kate has always seemed to me one of the most extra-ordinary things I have come across or known of in life, so considerably and astonishingly gifted a personality, so dominantly conspicuous an outcrop of the spiritual world, and yet so little known to, or apparently affecting the world, beyond—so far as I know—more than perhaps a score of persons now living.

I wonder whether she has left you any material which you could put on record for those who could appreciate and understand it. Her literary talent was dazzling.[30]

Winsten in *Salt and His Circle* reports that after J. R. MacDonald became Prime Minister, he asked Shaw for suggestions for the Honours List. According to Winsten, Shaw suggested Salt in a half-serious, half-jesting way.

Winsten then gives this Shaw quotation, perhaps from a letter to the Prime Minister, recommending Salt as "a man who would be perfectly at home among his old Eton friends in the Lords. He was a good dancer, a splendid Fives player, and the biggest authority in the world on wild flowers, a splendid qualification for a backwoodsman. He is a poor man so you will have to give him a sinecure like the Ministry of War or Secretary of State for India. If you want a man who could get on with Gandhi he is the man for you."[31]

Winsten says that MacDonald might have followed Shaw's suggestion but that the Prime Minister was informed that Shaw had been making disparaging remarks about him, and as a result he awarded the peerage to Olivier, who was then named Secretary of State for India.[32] The story has an apocryphal ring to it and can not be confirmed in the biographies of Shaw. Winsten may have had the story from Shaw, however, and the events may have happened as Winsten reported them. Salt did write Olivier in January of 1924, after Olivier's appointment as Secretary of State for India had been announced: "That was terrific news, almost too much for your septuagenarian friends, when coming on them so suddenly! I was doubly glad; on your behalf, and also for the land of my birth, now in such good hands.

"The whole business is like a dream, when one thinks of Hyndman and Morris with their little crew in the 'eighties."[33]

Lord Olivier also wrote an introduction to Salt's quiet pamphlet entitled *The Heart of Socialism,* published by the Independent Labour Party in 1927. Though Salt broke with the Fabians over the Boer War, he did not put aside his belief in the ethical and logical rightness of socialism. Lord Olivier felt that Salt's humor and irony were perhaps too subtle for the general reader. Perhaps that was so, but the pamphlet is convincingly done and notable because it does not deal with the internecine wars of the socialists but with the justifications for a humane redistribution of wealth.

In his long years of literary work, Salt met and corresponded with a large number of writers and critics. Many of these friendships were lasting. When he was writing his biography of Thoreau in 1889, he corresponded with William Sloane Kennedy, a friend of Whitman's. Salt's letters before 1920, except the initial one in 1889, are missing, but those for the years 1920 to 1929 (the year of Kennedy's death) have survived and are filled with items of literary interest. Salt wrote in detail about the reception of his own books, about Edward Carpenter and W. H. Hudson, and about his part in advancing Melville's reputation in England. Salt wrote of *Moby-Dick* in a letter of February 15, 1921, ". . . I think the 'Whale' is his chief work, in spite of its many faults, transcendentalism, &c. I introduced it to William Morris's notice, and he truly enjoyed it. So did Robert Buchanan, & others; but somehow Melville does not 'catch on', even in 'Typee' which is of course the most artistic of his books."[34] Salt also wrote to Kennedy of his own busy schedule, even though he was in his seventies, of botanizing in the summer and writing in the winter. The letters are consistently informative and entertaining.

To the Thoreauvian Dr. Samuel A. Jones of Ann Arbor, Michigan, Salt wrote over a hundred cards and letters, mostly about Thoreau. Salt listened carefully to Jones's criticism of the 1890 Thoreau biography, and followed many of his suggestions in the revised edition. He also sent Jones bibliographic items from English periodicals, looked up Thoreau items in the British Museum for him, and acted as a friendly critic of his works. The correspondence demonstrates Salt's openness, his willingness to take criticism, and to give criticism, tactfully.

Salt had corresponded with Melville, asking permission to reprint *Typee* in the Camelot Series published by Walter Scott. John Murray refused to allow the reprint, Melville informed Salt on February 25, 1890, though the novelist wanted to have the novel appear in that series.[35] In 1893, Salt wrote an introduction which appeared in Murray's editions of *Typee* and *Omoo*. He praised *Typee* as the best work in Melville's early period but considered *Moby-Dick* "the crown and Glory" of Melville's later phase: "less shapely and artistic than 'Typee,' it surpasses it in immensity of scope and triumphant energy of execution." In *Moby-Dick,* Salt went on, ". . . we see Melville casting to the winds all conventional restrictions and rioting in the prodigality of his imaginative vigour. . . ."[36] Salt had reservations about the overly Transcendental sections of the novel, and he was critical of the obscurity and mannerisms in *Mardi, Pierre,* and *The Confidence Man.* Salt's introduction is a perceptive sketch and leads one to regret that he did not write, as he once planned to do, a critical study of Melville.

Salt's literary work also brought him into contact with George Meredith, Algernon Swinburne, and, inevitably, Theodore Watts-Dunton. Salt saw at first hand how Watts-Dunton influenced Swinburne's literary opinions, and Salt wrote convincingly of Watts-Dunton's control over Swinburne. Salt's relationships with Meredith were more profitable; not only did Meredith help him with the *Life of James*

Thomson, but he also spoke freely to him of social and literary matters and agreed with him that the drift of Meredith's work was toward simplicity even though the novels had aristocratic and artificial settings.[37]

In *Seventy Years Among Savages* and *Company I Have Kept* Salt recorded his friendships with those who supported the humanitarian movement: Howard Moore, author of *The Universal Kinship;* Clarence Darrow; Ernest Crosby, the Tolstoyan; G. W. Foote, the rationalist; Ouida; and many others. He also knew Prince Kropotkin and other anarchists and corresponded with Tolstoy, though the letters do not seem to have survived.

THE LAST YEARS

After Kate's death in 1919, Henry was lonely and depressed. He retired from humanitarian work but kept busy with nature study and with his writing. There were few literary contacts, and his life was made miserable by Kate's terrible-tempered Russian protegée, who stayed on with him. In a letter to Kennedy of February 10, 1927, Salt said they had not gotten along well, for she was the most difficult person he had ever met, and that he had finally gotten rid of her by giving her a large part of his income.[38] In 1927, within a short time after the departure of the Russian woman, who is not referred to by name in the surviving correspondence, he married Catherine Mandeville, his housekeeper, and it was by all accounts a happy marriage. Shaw wrote on June 30, 1927, congratulating Salt on the marriage.[39]

Salt wrote Kennedy on March 30, 1927, that he had found "a most affectionate and devoted" companion and had feathered his nest for old age.[40] His happy marriage seems to have inspired him to write even more prolifically, and within the next years he published his translation of the *Aeneid, Our Vanishing Wildflowers, Memories of Bygone Eton, Company I Have Kept, Cum Grano,* and *The Creed of Kinship.* His last books received consistently good press notices, but few of them were bought. When Joseph Ishill wanted to publish him, Salt warned that he was not marketable.[41]

He kept writing almost to the end of his life. He wrote Edward Garnett in 1936 that he was doing a book entitled *The Philosophy of Failure* which would include material too "improper" for his accounts of Shaw, William Cory, Carpenter, and others.[42] Unfortunately, that book did not appear and the manuscript seems to have disappeared.

Although Salt was acutely aware of the failure of the Humanitarian League, and of his own failures, he did receive in the last decade of his life extraordinary praise from Gandhi. After writing Gandhi in September of 1929, Salt wrote this brief poem:

INDIA IN 1930

An India governed, under alien law
    By royal proclamation,
By force, by pomp of arms, that fain would awe
    Her newly-wakened nation;
While he who sways the heart of Hindustan,
    To more than kingship risen,
Is one old, powerless, unresisting man,
    Whose palace is—a prison.[43]

When Gandhi came to England in 1931, he gave a speech on November 20 at a meeting of the London Vegetarian Society. Salt was present and was especially honored by Gandhi's opening remarks: "When I received the invitation to be present at this meeting," Gandhi began, "I need not tell you how pleased I was, because it revived old memories and recollections of pleasant friendships formed with vegetarians. I feel especially honoured on my right Mr. Henry Salt. It was Mr. Salt's book, *A Plea for Vegetarianism,* which showed me why, apart from a hereditary habit, and apart from my adherence to a vow administered to me by my mother, it was right to be a vegetarian. He showed me why it was a moral duty incumbent on vegetarians not to live upon fellow-animals. It is, therefore, a matter of additional pleasure to me that I find Mr. Salt in our midst." Gandhi concluded his speech with another mention of Salt, who had been a member of the Society for over forty years. [44]

Almost a year after receiving those words of praise from one of the most famous men of the twentieth century, Salt wrote Gandhi:

Since I had the honour of meeting you in November last I have often thought of writing to you; and being now an octogenarian, and my life drawing near its close, I will no longer delay. I have the more reason to write because I wish to express to you the sympathy and admiration with which I have read of your recent efforts for the welfare of India.

The subject under special consideration, when I saw you in London, was Vegetarianism; and I feel as strongly as ever that food-reform, like Socialism, has an essential part to play in the liberation of man-kind. I cannot see how there be any real and full recognition of Kinship, as long as men continue either to *cheat,* or to *eat,* their fellow-beings![45]

Gandhi wrote these notes at the top of the letter: "I thank you for your letter. May I say in all humility that one rarely finds people outside India recognizing nonhuman beings as fellowbeings. Millenium [*sic*] will have come when mankind generally recognises and acts up to this grand truth. Thank you."[46]

A few other people remembered Salt during the 1930s. Shaw continued to write to him, but the two did not meet. John and Agnes Davies visited the Salts and corresponded with Salt during the last years of his life. Salt's letters were informative and amusing, even in his old age. In 1929 he wrote Mrs. Davies: "G. B. S. has been very kind and gracious about the Virgil. He sent me a copy of his 'Intelligent Woman's Guide to Socialism', and I was so fortunate as to find a mistake (grammatical) in it, for which he was quite grateful. He says it will prove the copy to be a First Edition, which, by 1950, or thereabouts, will be of immense value. He now advises me strongly to sell his letters; that 'no man who expects to leave a widow can afford not to sell.' "[47] And indeed Salt did sell and used the proceeds to help buy a house, which he called "The Shaw." In his witty, ironic letters to Mr. and Mrs. Davies, he wrote at length about rationalism, Shelley, Thoreau, euthanesia, and the failure of the Humanitarian League. He also maintained his close friendship with Bertram Lloyd, the pacifist, whose anthologies, *Poems Written During the Great War* and *The Paths of Glory,* showed, Salt believed, "that the conventional 'glory' of war is nothing but a mischievous illusion."[48] The radical minister Conrad Noel, whom Salt had first known as a schoolboy, wrote in his *Autobiography* that Salt "apologized for the unconscionable time he took in dying; with a smile he said: 'I am afraid the police will have me up for loitering.' "[49]

Although plagued by ill health and burdened by the failure of the Humanitarian League, Salt nevertheless was not in despair. He summed up his humanitarian principles in *The Creed of Kinship:*

(1) That our present so called "Civilisation" is only a "manner of speaking," and is in fact quite a rude state as compared with what may already be foreseen.

(2) That the basis of any real morality must be the sense of Kinship between all living beings.

(3) That there can be no abiding national welfare until the extremes of Wealth and Poverty are abolished.

(4) That Warfare will not be discontinued until we have ceased to honour soldiering as heroic.

(5) That the Rights of Animals have henceforth to be considered; and that such practices as cruel sports, vivisection, and flesh eating are not compatible with civilised life.

(6) That Free Thought is essential to progress, and that the religion of the future will be a belief in a Creed of Kinship, a charter of human and sub-human relationships.[50]

Salt wrote Agnes Davies in 1935 that *The Creed of Kinship* had been hurried into type "with the intention (I guessed) of showing it to Shaw complete and so having a better chance of getting a preface from him. But he has been very ill . . . and evidently has *not* acceded to his publisher's suggestion."[51] Shaw did not write the preface, but Salt was not distressed. He knew that he was better off without it, for Shaw's views would have clashed with his own and if Shaw had written an introduction everyone would have read Shaw, not Salt. "As it is," Salt wrote Mrs. Davies, "I may get attention from a handful of people, and Constables' can bear the loss from the book!"[52]

Salt did indeed have only a few readers, and he died in obscurity three years after the publication of this last work.

Catherine Salt wrote Shaw on May 30, 1939, the details of
Salt's death the previous week: He had begun having "brain
storms" four years before, she wrote, and she had stayed with
him constantly. Three weeks before he died, she had to enter
hospital for an operation. "I made," she wrote, "the best
arrangements I could for him but he became unmanageable &
they took him away to Hospital the day before he died. It's
that I can't get over. I had worked so hard & struggled &
fought to keep him in his own home & then to have to leave
him to die among strangers."[53]

Salt published in *Cum Grano* his "Epitaph on a Humanitarian," which looked to his own death:

> Here pause, in memory of a man
>   Less careful than most are
> To 'scape the fashionable ban
>   On such as 'go too far'.
> For him, Religion was the vow
>   To work no creature's ill:
> Folk groaned, 'He goes too far.' And now
>   He *has* gone—farther still.[54]

Did Salt go too far? He certainly devoted his energies to
causes which were misunderstood and unpopular. He was
vice-president of the Vegetarian Society; propagandist-
journalist for socialism and rationalism; for thirty years the
guiding spirit of the Humanitarian League.

Salt was a man of letters with a vast bibliography, and he
deserves more recognition than he has previously received.
Stephen Winsten in *Salt and His Circle* overemphasized Salt's
connections with Shaw, and while that relationship was important for both men, Salt had a vital life of his own. Salt's

work for the conservation of natural areas and of wild flowers, for better treatment of animals, for more humane prisons, for a more equitable economic system all show the breadth of his vision. His humane view of the kinship of all living things and his sympathetic concerns for literature were strongly influenced by the philosophies of Shelley and Thoreau, and his literary studies of these two writers are still of value.

With moral passion, sympathy, and understanding, Salt recorded the triumphs, the cruelties, the hypocrisies of the world. With logic, rhetoric, and wit, he attempted to change many of the baser ideas and practices of man. He failed, but he was able to retain a remarkable vision of a better world to come.

NOTES

1. Bernard Shaw, *Collected Letters: 1898–1910,* ed. Dan H. Laurence (New York: Dodd, Mead, 1972), pp. 489–90.

2. Edward Carpenter to Kate Salt, Nov. 24, 1890, Carpenter Collection.

3. K. Salt to Carpenter, Dec. 16, 1890, Carpenter Collection.

4. Bernard Shaw, preface to Stephen Winsten, *Salt and His Circle* (London: Hutchinson, 1951), p. 9.

5. *Ibid.,* p. 10; Bernard Shaw, *Getting Married* (New York: Brentano's, 1911), p. 233; Bernard Shaw, *The Millionairess* (New York: Dodd, Mead, 1936), pp. 150–51; Archibald Henderson, *George Bernard Shaw* (New York: Appleton-Century-Crofts, 1956), p. 544.

6. Winsten, *Salt and His Circle,* p. 215.

7. Henderson, *George Bernard Shaw,* pp. 801–2.

8. K. Salt to Carpenter, Jan. 28, 1899, Carpenter Collection.

9. Shaw, *Collected Letters: 1898–1910,* p. 16.

10. See Shaw's letter to Frank Harris in Harris's *Bernard Shaw* (London: Victor Gollancz, 1931), p. 238.

11. St. John Ervine, *Bernard Shaw: His Life, Work, and Friends* (New York: William Morrow, 1956), p. 315.

12. Bernard Shaw, *You Never Can Tell,* in *Plays Pleasant* (New York: Penguin, 1946), p. 258.

13. *Ibid.,* p. 285.

14. *Ibid.,* pp. 262, 296.

15. *Ibid.,* p. 297.

16. *Ibid.,* p. 300.

17. *Ibid.,* p. 344.

18. *Ibid.,* pp. 347–48.

19. Shaw, *Collected Letters: 1898–1910,* p. 340.

20. Quoted in Henderson, *George Bernard Shaw,* p. 418.

21. Shaw, *Collected Letters: 1898–1910,* pp. 46–47.

22. Carpenter to K. Salt, June 8, 1898, Carpenter Collection.

23. Catherine Mandeville Salt to G. B. Shaw, May 30, 1939, British Library, published with the permission of C. M. Salt.

24. Shaw to H. S. Salt, quoted in Winsten, *Salt and His Circle,* pp. 136–37. The original is at the New York Public Library.

25. H. S. Salt, ed., *Killing for Sport* (London: G. Bell, 1914), p. xii.

26. H. S. Salt to Shaw, Feb. 1, 1939, British Library. Published with permission.

27. K. Salt to Carpenter, Feb. 17, 1897, Carpenter Collection.

28. K. Salt to Carpenter, Nov. 3, 1900, Dec. 27, 1901, Carpenter Collection.

29. Henry S. Salt, "A Sage at Close Quarters," in *Edward Carpenter: In Appreciation,* ed. Gilbert Beith (London: George Allen & Unwin, 1931), pp. 198–99.

30. *Sydney Olivier: Letters and Selected Writings,* ed. Margaret Olivier (London: George Allen & Unwin, 1948), p. 147.

31. Winsten, *Salt and His Circle,* pp. 143–44. I am unable to verify this quotation.

32. *Ibid.,* p. 144.

33. *Sydney Olivier,* p. 156.

34. Quoted in Hendrick, "Literary Comments in the Letters of Henry S. Salt to W. S. Kennedy," p. 26.

35. Merrell R. Davis and William H. Gilman, *The Letters of Herman Melville* (New Haven, Conn.: Yale University Press, 1960), p. 294.

36. Henry S. Salt, introduction to Herman Melville, *Typee* (London: John Murray, 1893), p. xvi.

37. Henry S. Salt, *Seventy Years Among Savages* (London: George Allen & Unwin, 1921), p. 110.

38. H. S. Salt to Kennedy, Feb. 10, 1927, Rollins College Library.

39. Shaw to H. S. Salt, June 30, 1927, University of Texas and Berg Collection. The original is in the Berg Collection.

40. Hendrick, "Literary Comments in the Letters of Henry S. Salt to W. S. Kennedy," p. 27.

41. *A Group of Unpublished Letters by Henry S. Salt to Joseph Ishill.* See especially pp. 12, 17, 20.

42. H. S. Salt to Edward Garnett, Jan. 12, 1936, University of Texas Library, published with permission.

43. Henry Salt, *Cum Grano: Verses and Epigrams* (Berkeley Heights, N.J.: Oriole Press, 1931), p. 119.

44. *The Collected Works of Mahatma Gandhi* (Ahmedabad: Navajivan Press, 1971). XLVIII, 326.

45. H. S. Salt to Gandhi, Oct. 8, 1932, Gandhi National Museum and Library, New Delhi, published with permission.

46. *Ibid.*

47. H. S. Salt to Agnes Davies, Feb. 11, 1929, Pontin/Salt collection.

48. Henry S. Salt, *Company I Have Kept* (London: George Allen & Unwin, 1930), p. 176.

49. Conrad Noel, *Autobiography* (London: J. M. Dent, 1945), p. 21.

50. Henry Salt, *The Creed of Kinship* (London: Constable, 1935), p. viii.

51. H. S. Salt to Agnes Davies, Jan. 27, 1935, Pontin/Salt collection.

52. *Ibid.*

53. C. M. Salt to Shaw, May 30, 1939, British Library, published with permission.

54. Salt, *Cum Grano,* p. 146.

A LOVER OF ANIMALS.

AN ORIGINAL PLAY IN ONE ACT.

DRAMATIS PERSONAE:

DR. CLAUD KERSTERMAN.—Hospital surgeon; thirty-five, tall, dark, sallow, cynical.

TOM KERSTERMAN.—Younger brother of the above; a sportsman; rough, thickset, awkward.

MISS MOLL.—Aunt of the above; stout, dressy, fussy, loquacious.

GRACE GOODHART.—Companion to Miss Moll; about twenty-five, frank, open, decisive manner.

HACKET.—A butcher; bluff, ruddy, taciturn.

MRS. HACKET.—Dr. Kersterman's landlady; thin, prim, acrimonious.

PATE.—Servant to Dr. Kersterman; short, deformed, half-witted—wears black skull cap.

SCENE:

Dr. Kersterman's Parlour in Mrs. Hacket's House.

KERSTERMAN *is standing back to fire*—PATE *clearing the table after lunch.*

KER.—Pate.

PATE.—Yes, sir?

KER.—Is everything ready? Have you done all I told you?

PATE.—Yes, sir.

KER.—I expect these visitors almost immediately. Have you cleared up in my study?

PATE.—Cleared up what, sir?

KER.—What? Why everything—instruments, specimens—all that mess—odds and ends of every sort.

PATE.—Oh, yes. I did all that last night.

KER. (*after a pause*).—You understand, Pate, that during Miss Moll's visit none of these things are to be mentioned? Not a word—not a syllable—about them. You understand me?

PATE.—All right, sir.

KER.—Miss Moll is a great "lover of animals," and for the next day or two, while she's here, we're *all* to be lovers of animals. You see?

PATE (*uneasily*).—If I might ask the question, sir, what *is* a "lover of animals"?

KER.—Ah, there you have it, Pate! Well, I suppose it's a person who spends a lifetime on pampering cats and lapdogs.

PATE.—I suspect, sir, a "lover of animals" is much the same as them "anti-vivisectionists" I've heard tell of?

KER. (*half-aside*).—That's it. One of the old women who shriek if you prick a rabbit with a needle to save a man's life.

PATE (*going*).—Ah, if they only knew how *my* life was saved!

KER.—Yes, Pate. I couldn't have done it if I'd had to think of lap-dogs and rabbits. Just ask Mrs. Hacket to step up here a moment, will you?

[*Exit* PATE.

KER. *(looking after him).*—Now I do hope the fellow's confounded head won't give way while they're here. It'll be a pretty business if he blabs out something to the old woman; or to the young one either, for that matter. *(A knock)* Come in!

Enter MRS. HACKET.

KER.—Good afternoon, Mrs. Hacket. I wanted to be quite sure that everything's ready for these ladies. I expect them every minute now.

MRS. HACKET.—Yes, Dr. Kersterman, I shall be able to make them comfortable for the night, I hope. There are two of them, I believe?

KER.—Yes; Miss Moll (my aunt), and a Miss Goodhart, who lives with her and acts as "companion." . . . Oh, ah, yes, and there's "Prince." I forgot to mention him, though he's about the chief member of the party. He's Miss Moll's lapdog, you know. She writes that she'll probably bring "Prince," and perhaps her cat, "Selina."

MRS. HACKET *(with asperity).*—Now, Dr. Kersterman, sir, you must excuse my saying that I ought to have heard of this before. It's all against my rules to take in cats or dogs. Nasty dirty things, they bring fleas into the house, and spoil the chairs and furniture.

KER.—Come, come, Mrs. Hacket, be a good soul, and make an exception this time. I have most particular reasons for wishing Miss Moll's visit to go off pleasantly, and as she's a great lover of animals, I want her to feel that we're *all* lovers of animals here. It's only for a couple of days, you see. The fact is, as I hinted to you before, she's a well-to-do lady, and I'm expecting a large allowance from her shortly—she's coming to talk of business matters to-day—but it will be useless to hope for a penny of her money unless her cat and dog have a royal reception. It bears on the question of my rent, you see

. . . And this reminds me of something important. I am most anxious that neither my aunt nor her companion should hear a word about—my professional duties, you know—what I do in the interests of scientific research.

MRS. HACKET.—I'd been meaning to speak to *you* about that, Dr. Kersterman. There have been more complaints of late. I do wish you'd keep that nasty work for your laboratory, and not bring odd jobs of it here. Those frogs—

KER.—More complaints, indeed! And pray, who have complained now? I'd have them know I've got my licence, and can do what I like.

MRS. HACKET.—The neighbours talk, Dr. Kersterman. And Hacket don't like it, no more than I do. Poor things; it does seem shameful cruel to use them in that fashion.

KER. (*sneering*).—Ah, Hacket's business makes him so fond of animals, of course. All the same, you'd better not tell Miss Moll that he's a butcher. She's one of those who enjoy their cutlet without asking questions about where it comes from.

MRS. HACKET (*angrily*).—You may joke sir, but there's no more merciful man living than Hacket; and I'd have you know an honest butcher's as good as any scientific gentleman of *your* sort. Leastways he pays his debts, *he* does, and doesn't go trying to get other people's money by pretending to be a "lover of animals," and what not! Prince, indeed! Bringing beastly lap-dogs to this house, while your rent's owing for more than three quarters!

KER.—But, my good woman, it's just this visit of Miss Moll's that will enable me to *pay* my rent.

MRS. HACKET (*emphatically*).—I say to Hackett——
    [*Loud knocking. Exit* MRS. HACKET, *hurriedly.*

KER. (*grimly*).—They've come. Now for aunts, companions, cats, lap-dogs, and love of animals. It won't kill me for a couple of days, perhaps. Thank God, that scamp Tom's away. I'll steal a march on *him,* anyhow.

Enter MISS MOLL, *ceremoniously ushered in by* PATE *and* MRS. HACKET. *She is much dressed, and wears a large plume in her hat. She is followed by* GRACE GOODHART, *carrying a dog-basket.*

MISS MOLL.—Well, Claud, dear boy, here we are at last! So glad to see you again! Here's Prince, you see. He's sneezed several times on the journey, and I fear he's caught cold, but you'll prescribe for him, won't you? That'll be quite in your line, helping dumb animals. And Miss Goodhart—I mustn't forget her—you've seen her before haven't you, Claud?

KER.—Oh, yes, Aunt. Miss Goodhart and I are old acquaintances *(they shake hands).* But come; you must be tired. Mrs. Hacket will show you and Miss Goodhart your rooms, and then we will see what can be done for Prince. And Selina—where's Selina, aunt?

MISS MOLL *(gravely).*—I am sorry to say, Claud, that I've not been able to bring Selina, as I intended. I know you would have liked to have her here. But she had a bad attack of indigestion this morning, and could not possibly travel.

KER. *(sympathetically).*—Indeed, Aunt Moll, that's a great disappointment, both to Mrs. Hacket and myself.

MRS. HACKET *(eruptively).*—I must beg, sir,——

KER.—Mrs. Hacket, will you show these ladies to their rooms?

[*Exeunt* MRS. HACKET, MISS M., MISS G.

PATE *(advancing confidentially).*—May I inquire, sir, is the *young* lady also a lover of animals?

KER. *(impatiently).*—Yes, yes, I suppose so. I told you

we're *all* lovers of animals—for the next day or two. Now, don't forget my instructions, or say anything before Miss Moll about—you know what I mean—my professional studies.

[*Exit* PATE.

Re-enter MISS MOLL, *without cloak and hat.*

MISS MOLL.—I think it will be best, Claud, if you and I have our talk now, at once, while Grace is unpacking the bags and making Prince comfortable. What a strange-looking servant you have, Claud! Why does he wear that skull-cap?

KER.—Oh, he's an odd little chap whose life I saved by an operation at the hospital. Trepanned him, you know, and it left him a bit queer in the head at times. He was very grateful; and as he'd got nothing to do, I took him as a sort of man-of-all-work. He's very useful to me, though not orna-mental, certainly.

MISS MOLL.—Just like you, Claud! always doing good to somebody. It makes me feel more sure than ever that I'm right in my choice. You've thought over the idea since you had my letter?

KER.—Yes, thanks, Aunt Moll. I think I can undertake the post, if you decide to establish the Home. But, of course, all the details have got to be thought out carefully.

MISS MOLL.—The first thing is to get the general idea settled. It has been the wish of my life to establish a Domestic Pets' Convalescent Home, and I have set apart a special sum for that purpose; but the difficulty is to find a thoroughly reliable physician to put at the head of it (*dropping her voice and drawing closer to him*). I'm so terribly afraid, Claud, of these inhuman, devilish *vivisectors*. It seems that they——

Enter PATE.

PATE.—If you please, sir, the gamekeeper's sent to know (*stops in confusion*) if you'll want another—rabbit—

KER. (*angrily*).—The gamekeeper?—No, no, you idiot. The game-*dealer,* you mean. Tell him I want nothing. (*Exit* PATE). You were just saying Aunt Moll——

MISS MOLL.—I was saying, Claud, that I must take all possible precautions to guard my Domestic Pets' Convalescent Home from those vivisecting ruffians, and that is one reason why I want to give *you* the post. Not only because you are my favourite nephew, but because you are so enthusiastic a lover of animals. (KER. *bows*). My offer is this. To make you visiting physician at the Home, with a salary of £500 a year. If all goes well, I shall leave you all my money when I die. Now what do you say to this, Claud? If agreed so far, we can discuss details afterwards.

KER.—What can I say, dear Aunt Moll, except to thank you from my heart for the generous—munificent—offer? I am at your service, of course; but I must warn you that on such terms you could get many a better man than myself.

MISS MOLL (*dotingly*).—Your modesty, Claud; you were always so modest—so unlike your brother Tom.—By the by, where is Tom at present?

KER.—Oh, he's away in the country, Aunt, for a day or two. Rabbit-shooting, I believe.

MISS MOLL (*severely*).—Ah,—rabbit-shooting. If Tom has become *cruel,* as well as idle, I confess I don't regret missing him. It is strange that two brothers should be so unlike as you and Tom. I should be sorry to trust an animal of mine to *his* tender mercies! Without going so far as Grace goes, I do think this "sport," as they call it, is horribly barbarous.

KER.—And how far does Miss Goodhart go, Aunt Moll?

MISS MOLL.—That's rather a sore point between Miss Goodhart and myself; in fact, I don't think I can keep her with me much longer. It seems to me she injures a good cause by being so *extreme*. Also she's no right, while she's in my service, to air her fads at my expense. She takes up with all sorts of wild theories; has been a Vegetarian *(with a laugh)* for two years, and declares it suits her admirably!

KER.—Well, she doesn't *look* anything worse, certainly. I suppose she means to do the thing thoroughly; she was always a very logical young person, I remember.

MISS MOLL.—She has "ideas," Claud; and women have no business to have "ideas." I tell her that Vegetarianism is not *scriptural;* but she won't attend to me in the least. Now, couldn't you, as a medical man, Claud, just show her the *impossibility* of such a diet? It might save me from having to get rid of her; and she's useful to me in many ways. Both Prince and Selina are fond of her, too.

KER.—Well, Aunt, of course I could demonstrate the impossibility of being a Vegetarian; but if she already *is* one, I'm afraid it wouldn't have much effect. These unscientific people are so confoundedly obstinate, you see.

MISS MOLL.—She's as obstinate as—

Enter GRACE GOODHART.

Ah, Miss Goodhart, I was just telling Dr. Kersterman how fond you are of Prince!

GRACE.—I came down to say that everything's settled in your room. Prince has gone to sleep in the big velvet armchair.

MISS MOLL.—The darling little creature! I'll go and sit with him a while. Did you give him the cold wing of chicken?

GRACE.—No. He's had a lot to eat to-day. I thought he'd be better without more.

MISS MOLL.—Nonsense, Grace; the dog must have what he wants. *He's* not a Vegetarian, please remember.

[*Exit* MISS MOLL.

KER. *(after a pause)*.—I'm glad to hear that Prince is so comfortable, Miss Goodhart.

GRACE.—Does your landlady like having dogs in her best chairs, Dr. Kersterman?

KER.—She'll be delighted, I'm sure. She's as much a lover of animals as I am.

GRACE.—But I don't know how much that is, Dr. Kersterman. I can't recollect that when I knew you some years ago you were very ardent in the cause.

KER.—We live and learn, Miss Goodhart. May I ask what is your own position on this subject of the rights of animals?

GRACE.—My "position" is a simple one. I am Miss Moll's "companion." I am lady-in-waiting to Miss Moll, Prince, and Selina.

KER.—But I understand from my aunt that your views are more advanced than hers—in fact, that you are a Vegetarian. Isn't that going rather far?

GRACE.—Far? for a "lover of animals," do you mean?

KER.—Yes. Surely you could be a lover of animals without being an ascetic?

GRACE.—Then you would show your love of animals by killing and eating them? Well, that's "love" of a certain kind, perhaps, but rather a curious kind, I should say. "Cupboard love," I should call it, rather!

KER.—But I observe that my aunt has no objection to her

beef and mutton. Isn't *she* a shining light in the cause? You don't deny that *she's* a genuine lover of animals, I suppose?

GRACE.—Being Miss Moll's salaried attendant, I can't well criticise her, can I?

KER.—Oh, between friends, you know. Besides, as I'm to be visiting physician to her Domestic Pets' Convalescent Home, I'm in a similar difficulty.

Enter PATE.

PATE.—If you please, sir, the lady upstairs would be glad if you'd go to see the little dog. He wants physic, she says.

KER.—Ah—Prince. I'd forgotten him. (*To* MISS GOODHART.) Excuse me for a minute or two. A foretaste of my professional duties, you see. (*To* PATE.) Pate, bring a chair up to the fire for Miss Goodhart.

[*Exit* DR. KERSTERMAN.

PATE (*ceremoniously adjusting the chair*).—Excuse me, Miss, but may I make bold to ask, are *you* a lover of animals, like the other lady?

GRACE.—Oh, yes, I suppose so, Mr. Pate. We're *all* lovers of animals in this house, are we not?

PATE (*knowingly*).—Yes, Miss. We're all lovers of animals—*for the next day or two*. Those are Dr. Kersterman's instructions.

GRACE (*surprised*).—For the next day or two? I don't quite see what you mean by that.

PATE (*mysteriously*).—Now if those anti-vivisectionists—hope you're not one, Miss—only knew how *my* life was saved!

GRACE (*interested*).—Ah!—and how was your life saved, Mr. Pate?

PATE (*pointing to his skull-cap*).—You must ask Dr.

183

Kersterman about *that*. *He* did it. And what I say, is how would Dr. Kersterman have had the needful knowledge, if he'd had to think of rabbits and lap-dogs, and hadn't been able to try a trick or two aforehand? No anti-vivisection humbug for me, Miss! I've undergone an operation myself, and am all the better for it.

[*Exit triumphantly.*

GRACE.—This is terrible. I must speak to Claud. He's playing a darker game than I suspected. "Convalescent Home," indeed! A nice sort of convalescence *his* domestic pets will have, if this is true.

Enter DR. KERSTERMAN.

KER.—Well, I can give a good report of our little patient. I've diagnosed his case, and was able to promise a speedy recovery. You can imagine his mistress's relief at the favourable verdict! We were just talking of my aunt, weren't we? You don't think much of her as a lover of animals, I fancy. (*A pause.*) Is anything the matter?

GRACE.—Dr. Kersterman—are you—a vivisector?

KER. (*after a pause, savagely*).—How dare you ask me that question? Is this your "position" that you spoke of, as my aunt's companion?

GRACE.—I have a right to ask that question of the visiting physician of the Domestic Pets' Convalescent Home.

KER.—You have no right to come between my aunt and myself on a private family matter. But perhaps you've some little plan of your own for the disposal of her money? (*Changing suddenly.*) Forgive me, Grace. I lost my temper for the moment. It would be mad of us to quarrel. Our interests are identical.

GRACE.—Our interests are very far apart, Dr. Kersterman, if what I suspect be true.

KER.—When you spoke, I was on the point of returning to that talk we had years ago, the year I first met you at my aunt's house.

GRACE.—It is useless to go back to that, Claud. I distrusted you even then; and *now*—!

KER.—You rejected me then, with some reason perhaps, as a raw young doctor with neither name nor money. Surely you will not reject me now—now that I have secured my aunt's favour, and shall be able to offer you a home?

GRACE.—A *home?* The "Convalescent Home," Claud? No, thank you! *I* will not be a "domestic pet."

KER.—Are you jesting? You cannot mean to let your insane humanitarian ideas stand in the way of our advancement?

GRACE.—Will you please answer my question, Dr. Kersterman. Are you——?

Enter MISS MOLL, *excitedly.*

MISS MOLL.—Grace, come quickly! I want your help at once. Prince is sick. Claud, you must prescribe again, please.

KER. *(in a moment of supreme forgetfulness).*—Oh, damn Prince!

MISS MOLL.—Claud! Dr. Kersterman! Are you drunk, sir? Have you learnt your brother Tom's language?

KER.—Pardon me, Aunt Moll. I was worried about something else. I spoke without reflection.

MISS MOLL *(majestically).*—Miss Goodhart, we will leave this gentleman—to reflect.

[*Exeunt* MISS MOLL *and* GRACE.

185

Enter MRS. HACKET, *followed by* PATE.

MRS. HACKET.—Dr. Kersterman, something must be done at once about that beastly little dog, if your friends want to stay the night. He's spoilt the best velvet armchair, what belonged to Hacket's grandfather. I declare that I'll get Hacket to pole-axe him if you don't have him removed.

KER. *(in desperation).*—Oh, pole-axe the whole lot of them, by all means! Plague them all! I can stand it no longer. (*To* PATE.) You'll find me at the laboratory if I'm wanted.

[*Exit furiously.*

MRS. HACKET *(open-mouthed).*—What ever ails your master, Pate? He's gone off like an escaped bullock down a back alley, as Hacket would say.

PATE.—It's this "love of animals" business, I'll bet, Mrs. Hacket. The course of true love never *did* run smooth, I've heard.

MRS. HACKET.—Dr. Kersterman's "love of animals" don't exactly strike one as *true* love, either. The old lady's found him out, may be. Did you tell her anything, Pate?

PATE.—Not I; trust me. I had my instructions from the master.

MRS. HACKET.—Or the young lady? You told *her,* perhaps how Dr. Kersterman saved your life, and all the rest of that twaddling tale of yours?

PATE *(confused).*—Eh, well? And what if I did, Mrs. Hacket? What then, eh?

MRS. HACKET.—Oh, nothing—except that Kersterman's lost his allowance, and I've lost my rent. That's all, you idiot.

[*Exit* MRS. HACKET.

PATE *(standing dazed).*—Now, Lord bless me, if this "love of animals" ain't the cussedest thing out. We're all at loggerheads after scarce an hour of it, and a whole day more to run. It'll be the death of us all afore we've finished with it. *(A knock.)* Another caller! Who's the *next* lover of animals, I wonder?

Enter TOM KERSTERMAN *in shooting costume.*

TOM KER.—So Dr. Kersterman's not at home?

PATE.—No sir. He's at the laboratory. The ladies are upstairs, sir, with the little dog.

TOM KER.—Ladies? with the little dog? What the devil do you mean, Pate? Does Claud have lady students here, to watch his—

PATE.—Miss Moll is here, sir, with her lap-dog, Prince. We're all lovers of animals during her visit. Dr. Kersterman's instructions, sir.

TOM KER.—Whew! So *that's* the doctor's little game, is it? I've dropped in at the nick of time, it seems, for a nice little family meeting. Miss Goodhart here too, Pate?

PATE.—There's a young lady, sir, who carries the little dog, and looks after him when he's sick.

TOM KER.—I thought so. You needn't stay, Pate. And don't fetch your master just yet. I'll sit here till the ladies come down.

PATE *(opening the door).*—Here they are, sir.

Enter MISS MOLL *and* GRACE.

[*Exit* PATE.

TOM KER.—Good afternoon, Aunt Moll. I've just looked in on my way home, to see Claud, and find you instead. Shot at the pigeon, you see, and hit——An unexpected pleasure, I mean. Glad to see you, Miss Goodhart.

MISS MOLL *(haughtily).*—Good day, Tom. You've been

187

killing rabbits, I believe. Don't offer me your hand. There might be blood on it. (GRACE *shakes hands with* TOM KERSTERMAN.) Miss Goodhart, it appears, is not afraid of such contact.

GRACE.—I have been washing Prince, Miss Moll. If you were to do that yourself, other things might seem easier.

MISS MOLL (*severely*).—I hope to release you from that duty, Miss Goodhart, at an early date. (*To* TOM KERSTERMAN.) You must excuse my not appreciating your sporting instincts, Tom. I am a lover of animals, and am here to-day on a merciful errand—to appoint your brother, Dr. Kersterman, who fully shares my feelings, visiting physician to my Domestic Pets' Convalescent Home. You would hardly understand our objects, I fear.

TOM KER. (*bluntly*).—Well, aunt, I understand *Claud's* objects plain enough. He *has* made a fool of you this time, and no mistake!

MISS MOLL.—You are impertinent, sir. If you have nothing more sensible to say, you had better leave us. I am sorry that a nephew of mine should stoop to killing animals for sport.

TOM KER.—I don't cut 'em up alive, Aunt, at any rate.

MISS MOLL (*distantly*).—Who does, Tom? who does?

TOM KER.—Oh, lots of people. The visiting physician to the Domestic Pets' Convalescent Home, for one.

MISS MOLL (*in consternation—after a pause*).—You shall be called to account for this, sir! You accuse your brother of being a vivisector! Shameful!

TOM KER.—Ask Pate—ask the landlady—

MISS MOLL (*ringing*).—I will, sir.

Enter PATE.

Where is Dr. Kersterman?

PATE.—At the laboratory, ma'am. I was to fetch him if wanted.

MISS MOLL.—First answer me a question, Pate; and think well before speaking. Is your master—Dr. Kersterman—a vivisector?

PATE (*in ruinous confusion*).—Not—not—not for the next day or two, ma'am. We're all lovers of animals, while you're here, ma'am. Dr. Kersterman's instructions, ma'am.

MISS MOLL.—That is quite enough, Pate. Fetch Dr. Kersterman at once; and tell Mrs. Hacket to come here.

[*Exit* PATE.

(*To* GRACE.) Did you know this Miss Goodhart?

GRACE.—I *suspected* it, for the first time, this afternoon.

MISS MOLL.—And did not tell me at once?

GRACE.—I was going to question Claud myself. You called me away to attend to Prince before I could learn the truth.

MISS MOLL.—"Claud" indeed! So *that* was the pleasant *tête-à-tête* I interrupted! I seem to have been pretty well fooled all round!

TOM KER. (*eagerly*).—That's just what I was saying, Aunt, when you called me impertinent.

MISS MOLL.—Hold your tongue, Tom. (MRS. HACKET *enters*). Mrs. Hacket, I must ask you a question about my nephew, Dr. Kersterman. Do you know if he is—a vivisector?

MRS. HACKET.—Good gracious, ma'am, what a question! I know nothing of my lodger's professional studies, ma'am. All I know is that Dr. Kersterman is a good deal behind with his rent, and that the armchair upstairs, what belonged to Hacket's grandfather, will have to be paid for. Hadn't you best ask Dr. Kersterman himself? I hear him coming.

TOM KER.—My eye! We're in for a fine shindy now!

Enter DR. KERSTERMAN *followed by* PATE.

KER. (*after a pause—looking round defiantly*).—All waiting for *me*, I see. You do me too much honour. Very good of you to look in, Tom. I owe this pleasant gathering to *you*, no doubt.

MISS MOLL.—Your brother has made a statement, Claud, which I trust you will instantly contradict. You must admit that, before appointing you Visiting Physician to my Domestic Pets' Convalescent Home, I am bound to ask whether you practise—I am almost ashamed to speak the word—whether you practise *vivisection*.

KER.—I will not be catechised and bullied like this. How much do any of you know of what you call "vivisection?" As a scientist I use the approved methods of science.

TOM KER.—Such as playing the "lover of animals" before Aunt Moll, for instance?

KER.—If you're insolent, Tom, I'll throw you out of the window. Precious lies you've been telling about me in my absence, it seems!

TOM KER. (*advancing angrily*).—And what lies had *you* been telling Aunt Moll in *my* absence? She treated me like a red-handed murderer when she came in.

KER.—Well, now you've turned informant, Tom, you've earned your reward. Hope you've made good terms with Aunt Moll.

TOM KER.—Liar! (*They come to blows*).

MISS MOLL.—Help! thieves! murder! (*To* MRS. HACKET).

Call your husband, woman! Fetch the policeman, Pate! Save Prince, Grace, quick!

MRS. HACKET (*running to the door*).—Hacket, Hacket! Come up at once! Just as you are—in your killing clothes—anyhow!

Enter HACKET, *in blue smock, bare armed.*

HACKET (*placing himself between the combatants*).—Now, which of you two gentlemen wants to be stuck like a pig? Who speaks first?

MISS MOLL.—What's this? A *butcher!* So you've brought me to a slaughter-house, Claud, as well as a den of vivisection! Grace, let us go at once. How horrible! A *butcher!*

MRS. HACKET.—Slaughter-house indeed! when Hacket does all his killing off the premises, quite respectable, at his shop! I'm sure our door's open for you to step out, ma'am, whenever you choose.

MISS MOLL.—We will leave your house, madam, immediately. Have you anything to say, Claud, before we go?

KER. (*recovering himself*).—This is ridiculous. Hands off, Tom! All right Hacket! Your pardon, Aunt Moll, for this blackguardly scene. (*After a pause.*) Yes, yes—if you *must* pry into my private affairs, I am what you call a "vivisector"—that's to say, I am devoting what knowledge and skill I possess to the good of my fellow creatures. As you ask for plain speaking, Aunt Moll, I tell you that this old-womanish crusade against science is mere maudlin sentiment. As Owen said, you are *bestiarians,* not humanitarians at all. Are you aware that all the great modern surgical discoveries are due to experiments on animals?

Miss Moll.—After calling me a "bestiarian," Claud, you can hardly suppose that I shall argue with you further.

Pate *(coming forward).*—Now, if you only knew, ma'am, how *my* life was saved—

Ker.—Well, take Pate's case, for instance—

Mrs. Hacket.—Oh, come, Dr. Kersterman, the less said about *that* poor creature, the better! All the neighbours know that his head was cut open for the sake of the students of the hospital, and not for his own benefit at all. And he's been an idiot ever since.

Ker. *(ignoring her).*—But if you must needs preach this gospel of "kindness to animals," why begin with vivisection? What of sport? Tom can tell you how the noble sportsman wounds thousands of wretched animals, left crawling and fluttering in the brushwood—and all for mere *pleasure,* mark you—not for knowledge, or any real profit to mankind. Yet you mildly lecture the sportsman, while you treat the scientist as a pariah.

Tom Ker.—That's all very fine, Claud; but you know sport makes us *manly.* What would Englishmen be without their national field-sports?

Ker.—Yes, *you're* a fine specimen, ain't you, of the manliness of rabbit shooting. Then again, Aunt, I don't quite see where your own "love of animals" comes in. You *eat* them, don't you? And your butcher, like our friend Hacket here, causes more pain than a hundred operators on animals.

Hacket.—Dr. Kersterman, sir, I'm a plain working man, but if it's love o' animals you're talking about, I yield to none. 'Twas because I was so fond of 'em as a lad, and liked to have 'em round me, that I took to the butchering trade. I'm never so content as when I'm in full swing o' business, and up to my

ankles in blood. But I'll say this, though I earn my livelihood
by killing animals, I wouldn't torture 'em as you do, not for
all the wealth o' carcases in Smithfield.

MISS MOLL (*sarcastically*).—So you're a convert to Vegetarian ideas, Claud! (*Looking at G.*) I can guess where you got
them from. And, perhaps, *you* agree with Dr. Kersterman,
Grace, as to the benefits of Vivisection? Extremes meet, you
know.

GRACE.—Your quarrel with your nephew, Miss Moll, is no
affair of mine. But as you've dragged me into this discussion,
I shall say what I think. I abominate Vivisection as the most
horrible of crimes—the more horrible just because it is done,
as Dr. Kersterman says, deliberately and conscientiously (we
must grant him that), and not from mere thoughtlessness,
like sport. But if we are to fight Vivisection, we must rid
ourselves of this false "love of animals," this pampering of
pets and lap-dogs by people who care nothing for the real
welfare of animals, or even for the welfare of men.
Humanitarianism must show that it is *not* "bestiarian," and
must aim at the redress of *all* needless suffering, human and
animal alike—the stupid cruelties of social tyranny, of the
criminal code, of fashion, of science, of flesh-eating. There! I
have said my say; and now it only remains for me to take my
departure and go.

MISS MOLL.—Take your departure, Miss Goodhart! And
how are Prince and I to get home, pray?

GRACE.—I will see you and Prince home, Miss Moll, but
we part company at your door.

MISS MOLL.—Well, of all bumptious hussies, commend
me to the forward young woman who has "ideas." Good-bye,
Claud; I'm going to pack up and be off. I trust you will seek

forgiveness where it is to be found. Of course I shall cancel all the arrangements that we talked of—for the Domestic Pets' Convalescent Home.

KER.—Good-bye, Aunt. I wish you and your domestic pets all happiness. Hope you'll find Selina in better health.

[*Exit* MISS MOLL.

TOM KER. (*coming forward*).—I'm going, Claud. We can talk this over another time. Now the old lady's off, we can afford to laugh a bit, can't we? It's clear you and I are in the same boat, as far as love of animals is concerned! Sorry to have caused this infernal row to-day. Good afternoon, Miss Goodhart.

KER.—All right, old chap. We'll get along somehow.

[*Exit* TOM KER.

MRS. HACKET (*after whispering with Hacket*).—After what's happened to-day, Dr. Kersterman, we must give you a week's notice. The rent will have to be paid before you go, of course. And there's that chair what belonged to——

KER.—Oh, of course, Mrs. Hacket. I'll sell my books if necessary. Leave me now.

MRS. HACKET (*going*).—Ah! your hands are empty, and your mouth full of promises—as usual!

[*Exeunt* H., *and* MRS. H.

GRACE.—Good-bye, Dr. Kersterman. I'd like you to know that *I*, at any rate, don't look on you as a "pariah," though I do think you are fatally wrong, heart and mind, in the course you've taken up. We are not likely ever to meet again. I'm sorry I came to-day.

KER.—Good-bye, Miss Goodhart. All my plans are broken; and you've lost your position, I fear, with Aunt Moll. What will you do when your duties to the lap-dog are concluded?

GRACE.—Oh, I shall find out a path for myself somewhere. Miss Moll and I were bound to part company before long, and it's as well the time has come quickly, the new ideas and the old can't work forever in company. Now we shall all know where we stand.

MISS MOLL (*from the doorway*).—Miss Goodhart! Grace! Come and help me to pack!

[*Exit* G.

KER. (*after a pause*).—Well, Pate, and what do *you* think of today's doings? Fine thing to be a lover of animals, isn't it?

PATE (*confidentially*).—Might I ask, is it necessary, sir, to be a lover of animals any longer?

KER.—No. It's all over now, Pate. The old lady's been too much for us. Game's up.

PATE (*ruefully*).—Ah, if only those "anti-vivisectionists" knew how *my* life was saved!

[*Exit* PATE.

KER. (*alone*).—So it seems there is just *one* person left who believes in me. And he is half-witted.

[CURTAIN]

B

THE HOME SECRETARY'S HOLIDAY.

A PRISON PLAY IN ONE ACT.

A prisoner, "B. 20," a man of sallow, lawyer-like appearance, looking about forty years old, is seated on a four-legged stool in the centre of a small cell, picking oakum.[1] *There is a door to the right, a ground-glass window to left, and at the back a small table and folded plank-bed. In the right-hand back corner is a small shelf, with one or two books of devotion, a brush and comb, soap, &c., and below it a bundle of bedclothing, small water-can and bowl. On the whitewashed wall hangs a printed card of Rules.*

B. 20 *(sighing, then speaking in a measured rhetorical tone).* A week to-day—a week still to run! Can I live through it? Fool, idiot that I was, ever to let myself in for this! Let me think—let me think—but how can one think—*here?* The brain reels with absolute vacuity. It seems an age already, and life small and far away, like something looked at through the wrong end of a telescope. *(A pause.)* And Blanche—what is *she* doing now, I wonder? She promised to bear it pluckily, dear girl: so don't let *me* play the coward. Well, I suppose if I've got through one week, I can survive another. I must brace

1. "Picking oakum" was make-work in English prisons at the time of this play. Used ropes were unravelled for the hemp fiber to be used as caulking material.—G.H.

myself up, and remember that I'm not here without a cause. (*Sings.*)

> "Stone walls do not a prison make
> Nor iron bars a cage."

THE WARDER (*a sour-looking fellow, with flushed face and sinister expression, opening the door suddenly from without*). B. 20, no more of that, I tell you. Keep your mouth shut, can't you? Singing ain't allowed. (*Glares sternly, and retires.*)

B. 20 (*quietly*).   Nothing *is* allowed here, it seems. Well, I'm having an experience, and no mistake! If my friends knew of it! It makes me laugh to think how horrified Gravely would be if it leaked out. But they mustn't know, that's certain. I must hold on, and crawl through it as I can. I am a prisoner, and must conduct myself as such. Ah! who comes now? The Governor!

(*As he rises, the Governor, Colonel Stark, enters—a tall, stern, eagle-eyed man, with grizzled hair, military bearing, and short laconic manner.*)

THE GOVERNOR.   Now, my man, what is it? I hear you have a complaint to make to me. Out with it.

B. 20 (*beginning a speech*).   I wish to make an appeal to you, sir, rather than a complaint, on a matter of personal cleanliness. My request is so entirely reasonable that I am sure you will not refuse it——

THE GOVERNOR.   Of course. They all say that. What is it?

B. 20.   When I came here, my tooth-brush and nail-scissors were taken from me with my other things, and I have repeatedly asked for them in vain.* Would it be in any way

---

* This and one or two other incidents in this Play are borrowed from Mr. F. Brockelhurst's "I was in Prison." [H.S.]

subversive of discipline if I were allowed to clean my teeth and finger-nails? Would it——

THE GOVERNOR *(kindly but firmly)*. Now look here, my good fellow. A word of caution. I judge from your appearance that you've known better days. An educated man, aren't you?

B. 20. I thought I was, sir, till I came here. But it seems that no education is complete until——

THE GOVERNOR *(motioning him to be silent)*. Until you have learnt to hold your tongue and obey rules. Where did you get this dreadful trick of talking? Of all the gifts a prisoner can have, the gift of the gab is the unhappiest. There are the Rules *(pointing)*. Study them. Ask no questions.

B. 20. But if the case be a special one——

THE GOVERNOR. Nonsense, sir. There are no special cases in this prison. *(Producing a note-book, and reading from it.)* "B. 20, George Tomkins, convicted of an attempt to defraud a Railway Company. Sentence, fourteen days." What is there special about that?

B. 20. Then I must appeal elsewhere, I suppose. It is impossible to believe that the Prison Board wishes prisoners to be dirty.

THE GOVERNOR *(drily; going)*. Ah, you would like to appeal to the Home Secretary, perhaps.

B. 20. I should. From all I have heard of him I am convinced that the Home Secretary would not wish me to be deprived of the common decencies of life.

THE GOVERNOR *(after curiously regarding him)*. Enough, sir. I cannot grant your request. For your own sake I recommend you to obey the Rules of the Prison. You have your work *(pointing to the oakum)*. Do it. *(Exit Governor.)*

B. 20 *(sitting down again to his work)*. Much good I have

done myself by appealing to *him!* Is it possible that these hide-bound military martinets are the men we set over our Prisons! But he's right in one thing: it's no use *talking,* with this pile of stuff to be unravelled. And perhaps other things to be unravelled also! *(Rising suddenly.)* But confound it! how can one work, when it's torture even to sit? I'm as stiff from this stool of penance as if I'd been on the rack. I must manufacture an extempore cushion, I suppose *(lays a quantity of oakum on the stool and re-seats himself)*. Perhaps I shall sit upon the Woolsack some day: this must serve meanwhile.

WARDER *(opening the door suddenly)*. B. 20, take the oakum off that seat, will you. It's against rules.

B. 20 *(after staring at him blankly for a moment)*. Why, of course it is, my good fellow! That's one of the things I might have guessed. All part of the great penal principle of *vœ victis!* *(Removing the oakum.)* Well, I must wait for the Woolsack, after all.

WARDER. Hold your jabber, I tell you, and don't let me have to warn you a second time. Woolsack, indeed! you'll get the sack from here to a punishment-cell, if you go on like this. *(Exit.)*

B. 20 *(holds up his hands in mute despair; then suddenly calls after the warder)*. Ho, there, officer!

WARDER *(re-entering, sternly)*. What is it now, B. 20? No more talk, I tell you, unless you want to be reported.

B. 20. I only wish to exercise my right as a prisoner, and to ask whether I can see the doctor, as I requested.

WARDER. Yes. Wait till he sends for you. *(Putting his head outside the door.)* Hush! the Visiting Justice is coming round. Get to work, I tell you. The Visiting Justice!

[*As B. 20 sits down to work, Mr. Prim, the Visiting Justice, is shown in by the Warder, who then retires. He is a smug, spry, spectacled old gentleman, of antique garb, and benevolent demeanour. He carries several books under his arm.*]

MR. PRIM.   Good day, my friend. I've just heard from the librarian that you'd been applying for a book, and couldn't get one to your taste; so I've brought a few with me for you to choose from. There is nothing more important for the reformation of a sinner than well-chosen reading.

B. 20.   It is extremely kind of you, sir. I need a book badly; for in this horrible cellular confinement the mind is thrown back, as it were, upon itself——

MR. PRIM.   Thrown back upon itself! Why, of course it is, my friend! That is just the value of our English penal system. Segregation—solitude—introspection—self-questioning—remorse—these are the heaven-sent means by which the sinner is awakened to a sense of his guiltiness.

B. 20.   You say "heaven-sent," sir. I should have thought it was altogether from the other quarter that this torment was invented.

MR. PRIM.   Hush, hush, my friend! This is wild and blasphemous talk. It is by this salutary discipline alone that the sinful mind can be purified. Turn your thoughts inward——

B. 20.   But, my dear sir, that's just where I've turned them till I'm on the verge of madness. I want to turn them not inward, but inside out. It is the sun, the air, the sky, the breath of life that the sinner needs—not this insufferable concentration on his own sinfulness. I've learnt that much, at any rate, since I've been in this death-trap. For God's sake give me a book!

MR. PRIM.   I will, my friend, I will. You shall have your

choice of several, and good, sound, instructive books they are. "Approved books of moral instruction" is the regulation phrase, you know. Here's one on "Criminological Principles," for example.

B. 20.   Are you jesting, sir? Do you suppose that, with this practical demonstration of criminological principles around me I want to refresh my mind by *reading* about them? Why, I've simply lived on criminology for the last seven days; my mind is sodden with it. Give me something logical to read, sir, or biological, or anthropological, or sociological, or zoological, or phrenological, or astrological—or even theological—but not criminological. I can't stand that.

MR. PRIM *(aside)*.   A strange character this! Where did he get his education from? *(To B. 20.)* Well, then, what do you say to these? Here's Smiles's "Self Help," "Holy Living and Holy Dying," Fox's "Book of Martyrs," and "The Lives of Twelve Good Men." All books of real moral instruction.

B. 20 *(ruefully)*.   Not a doubt of it, sir. I should say it would be a sort of real moral oakum picking to read them. *(Insinuatingly.)* Now, couldn't you get me something a bit more lively, sir? a novel, for instance?

MR. PRIM *(aghast)*.   A novel, my friend! You horrify me! Who has ever heard of a sinner's mind being roused by a novel?

B. 20.   Why, yes, indeed, sir. There are novels published nowadays that can make even the sinner "sit up," so to speak.

MR. PRIM *(shocked)*.   Enough, enough, sir! Your misplaced levity is most painful to me. Let me recall you to a sense of your very serious position. Turn your thoughts inward, I pray you. Introspection, solitude, remorse—these are—

[*Enter Warder.*]

WARDER (*to Mr. Prim*).   Beg pardon, sir, but the doctor wishes to see this prisoner at once.

MR. PRIM.   Very well, warder. (*To B. 20.*) I will await your return, my friend. I must have some further talk with you.

B. 20 (*going*).   Not inward talk, I hope, sir. Let me forget that poor skeleton in the cupboard that men call the conscience.

[*Exeunt B. 20 and Warder.*]

MR. PRIM.   Now, who can this strange man be, I wonder? His face seems to be known to me, and yet I can't remember how. I fear, I much fear, his thoughts are not directed where they should be.

[*Enter the Governor.*]

THE GOVERNOR (*sternly*).   Why is this door open?

MR. PRIM.   Good morning, Colonel. You've got a strange character here, I find.

THE GOVERNOR (*looking round the cell*).   Good morning, Prim. But we *haven't* got him, it seems. Where is he?

MR. PRIM.   With the doctor. So I'm waiting to give him some moral physic on his return. He needs it badly, Colonel.

THE GOVERNOR.   Who is the man? Has he told you anything? Do you see a likeness to anyone?

MR. PRIM.   I was just wondering, when you came in. He seems an exceptional sort of prisoner; but alas! it's the more difficult to awaken him to a sense of his condition.

THE GOVERNOR.   Oh, you'd better drop that, Prim, in this case. He's awake enough—very wide awake—I suspect. And his gift of the gab is something awful.

MR. PRIM(*hurt*).   But he's not awake to the right things, Colonel Stark, not to the eternal verities. Introspection, self-questioning, remorse—of these he will hear nothing.

THE GOVERNOR(*testily*).   Introspection be hanged! I tell you, Prim, I am troubled about the man. There's some mystery about his case. I hoped you might have learnt something; but all you do is to talk about awakening *him*. It's *we* who want awakening, I tell you, sir.

MR. PRIM.   But why this mystery, Colonel? Surely you have the details of the case?

THE GOVERNOR.   Of course, of course. But I tell you, in strict confidence, there's something unexplained about them. I have communicated with the Home Secretary.

MR. PRIM.   Ah, the Home Secretary! A well-meaning and conscientious minister, no doubt; but too impetuous, too quixotic, I fear, if all one hears is true, and married to a giddy, headstrong, sentimental young woman! What does he say, Colonel?

THE GOVERNOR.   He says nothing. The permanent officials say that the Home Secretary is away on a fortnight's holiday. (*Darkly.*) There's just the mischief of it.

MR. PRIM.   Well, my friend, then you must wait till he returns, I suppose. Patience is a virtue, you know.

THE GOVERNOR.   Spare me your virtues, Prim! It happens that by the time the Home Secretary is back, this man will be out.

MR. PRIM.   Well, what then, Colonel?

THE GOVERNOR.   What then? Why, this—

[*Re-enter B. 20, escorted by the Warder. They regard him curiously.*]

THE GOVERNOR (*to B. 20*).   Well, sir. What does the doctor say? Are the vocal organs affected?

B. 20.   He says that I'm suffering from nervous prostration, and must go into hospital to-morrow.

THE GOVERNOR.   Very well. You are now satisfied, I hope. Have you anything else to say to me?

B. 20.   Only about that matter of my tooth-brush and nail-scissors——

THE GOVERNOR.   They will be given you in the hospital. Anything else? *(looking hard at him).*

B. 20.   I hope you do not think I have been shamming to the doctor, sir? I would far rather have served out my time as an ordinary prisoner. I came here with that intent—I mean, I would rather have had the usual experience.

MR. PRIM.   But the time in hospital need not be wasted, my friend. There, no less than here, you can turn your thoughts inward—

B. 20 *(to Governor, losing patience).*   Could you not turn this gentleman outward, sir? His platitudes are harder to bear than the plank-bed itself. I cannot believe that the Rules *(pointing to the copy on the wall)* authorise this annoyance to prisoners.

THE GOVERNOR.   Silence, sir! Behave yourself; or you may go to a worse place than the hospital. Come, Mr. Prim. We must be going. *(Looking at his watch.)* There is a matter of discipline that demands my attention elsewhere.

MR. PRIM *(to B. 20).*   Good day, my friend, and God bless you! In spite of what you have said, I shall leave you "Criminological Principles" *(puts the book on table).* It will help you to control your thoughts, and realise your position. Introspection, my friend, self-questioning, remorse—these, and these alone——

THE GOVERNOR.   Come along, Prim, come along!

[*Exeunt Governor, Prim, and Warder.*]

B. 20.   The smug, sanctimonious, canting old humbug! "I was in prison, and ye came unto me." Poor prisoners and captives, indeed, if *these* are the sort of visitors we send them in their affliction. Well, well! a nice mess I've made of it, after all my fine resolutions! To go into hospital, to slink off on the sick list, after only seven days of it, while there are many who have to undergo it for months, for years, for life! But let me rest, let me rest! (*Letting down the plank-bed.*) I will try an interval of plank-bed and "Criminological Principles." (*Takes the book, and reads, lying down.*)

[*A slow, measured tapping is heard on the back wall.*]

B. 20 (*getting up, listening curiously, and tapping in response*).   Eh? Who's there? Yes, yes?

A VOICE (*faintly*).   Buck up, my lad! buck up! It won't last for ever!

B. 20.   Yes, yes! What is it? I'm listening.

WARDER (*entering suddenly*).   Now, look here, B. 20! You're breaking rules again. You're a-listening, are you? And what to, I'd like to know? And your bed down, out of regulation hours!

B. 20.   Oh, its nothing, warder, it's nothing. I was only talking to myself. The silence of this place is rather oppressive, you know. There's a good deal of talking in the life I'm accustomed to.

WARDER.   The silence, indeed! You'll be wanting next to have a grand piano in your cell, and some chamber music perhaps? What else but silence do you expect, if you get sent *here?*

[*Suddenly, from a remote part of the prison, a prolonged, agonizing, toneless screech is heard, followed by a complete hush.*]

B. 20 (*horror-stricken*).   Good heavens! What is that awful cry? What hellish thing is being done now?

WARDER (*with a grin, facetiously*).   Well I likes that, B. 20. Here you are complaining of the silence of this place; and the very moment you hear a bit of a song, you complain of that too. We can't satisfy you, nohow.

B. 20.   Song, song, do you call it! It was the most horrible heart-shaking sound I ever heard in my life. What on earth was it, man? For God's sake, tell me.

WARDER (*grinning*).   It's the tune as you'll be singing yourself, B. 20, if you don't mend your manners. That's how they generally sing, when they get two dozen with the cat. Now you just get to work, and behave yourself, or I'll report you afore this day's out.

[*Exit Warder, after replacing bed.*]

B. 20 (*beginning in a whisper, and raising his voice as he proceeds*).   How horrible—how unspeakably horrible and shocking! To think that that hyæna-like howl came from the throat of a fellow-being, a man made in God's image! And in an age when we pretend that torture has been abolished, and when it would be thought diabolical to burn a heretic at the stake! With such a sound in one's ears, what becomes of all the fine arguments they are for ever flourishing in Parliament and the press, about the need of brutal punishments for brutal prisoners, and the impossibility of degrading the degraded ruffian still further! Do not tell me that the thing that screeched like that has not been degraded below what he was before. Will it come again, I wonder? (*stopping his ears*). Ugh! I shall hear it and dream of it for the rest of my life. Let me read, let me calm myself, or I shall go mad. (*Sits down and tries to read "Criminological Principles": then, after a pause, starts up convulsively.*) Criminological Principles, forsooth! Words, words! What is the use of glossing over in books things that are intolerable in fact? (*Flings the book on the floor with a bang.*)

WARDER (*entering furiously, and seizing B. 20 by the collar*). So you're determined to have it, are you? I've warned you till I'm tired, and now I'm cussed if I don't report you for misconduct. Hospital indeed! It's the punishment cell you want, and you'll have it, too.

B. 20 (*utterly unnerved*). I can stand it no longer! Let me go, you brutal blockhead! Do you know who you're speaking to? (*a pause*). I'm the Home Secretary—yes, Sir Charles Windham, in disguise. There now—the secret's out.

WARDER (*laughing sardonically*). Oh, ay, B. 20, that's the style, is it? Are you sure you ain't the Archbishop o' Canterbury himself, while you're about it? Come, come, you impudent varmint, I've been a warder here eighteen years, and I've heard that sort of thing too often to be took in by the likes of you.

B. 20 (*recovering his self-possession*). Ah, yes, no doubt you have. Say nothing of it, warder, I beg of you. I was only joking, of course.

WARDER. Only joking, was you? You'll get the cat yourself, you will, when I tells the Governor your little joke. (*Opening the door and looking out.*) Why, here comes the Governor, post haste, and a whole party o' folks with him. (*With changed manner.*) What's up now, I wonder? My word!

[*Approaching steps are heard, and voices as if in argument and remonstrance.*]

B. 20 (*calmly*). Ah! It's all out, I see! I thought that would be the end of it! Well, I must brave it out, I suppose. Here they come, and no mistake.

[*The door is opened by the warder, who stands dumfounded. Lady Windham, a handsome and recklessly romantic young lady, rushes into the cell, closely followed by Mr. Gravely, who is trying to*

*detain her, and the Governor, whose countenance is grim and stern,
but with a twinkle of humour in his eye. Mr. Gravely, a Permanent
Secretary of the Home Office, is a long-faced heavy-moustached
official, a pattern of respectability both in dress and demeanour.*]

B. 20.   Why—Blanche! Is it possible? And you,
Gravely!

LADY WINDHAM *(embracing B. 20)*.   My dear, dear Charlie! Now don't, don't scold me! It really wasn't my fault. I
couldn't keep the secret a minute longer, and Mr. Gravely had
found it all out at the Office, and said we must come and
release you immediately. So we've come, you see!

MR. GRAVELY.   We have, indeed! Are you aware, Lady
Windham, that your intrusion into this part of the prison is
an unprecedented breach of regulations?

B. 20.   My dear Blanche, I have not the slightest reason
for scolding anyone but myself. I've been a fool, and must
take the consequences.

LADY WINDHAM.   A fool! I call it glorious, Charlie, and
so romantic too! Why, I declare the dress suits you beautifully! And what a dear little room you've got! It's so simple,
yet so cosy. *(To the Governor.)* I'm so devoted to simplicity of
living, Colonel Stark. I'm a great reader of Thoreau and
Edward Carpenter, you know. Are all your rooms as neat as
this one?

THE GOVERNOR *(grimly)*.   Much the same pattern,
madam. We do things methodically under the Prison Board.
(To B. 20.) I beg you to note, Sir Charles, or B. 20, if you
prefer that name, that I can no longer be responsible for
discipline in this prison *(pointing to Lady Windham)*.

MR. GRAVELY.   The whole incident has been improper
to an unheard of degree. All we can now hope is that the Press
will not get hold of it.

LADY WINDHAM. Oh, that will be all right, Mr. Gravely. We are all friends here, you know. (*Looking round at the warder, who stands open-mouthed at the door.*) I suppose you've been Sir Charles's attendant, have you not? You worship him, of course, as all the servants do?

WARDER (*confusedly*). Oh, yes, Mum: yes, yes, your Leddyship, yes, certainly. Anything I can do, Mum—at your service, lady.

LADY WINDHAM (*to B. 20*). He has been very good to you, Charlie, I feel certain. I told Mr. Gravely, as we came down, that I quite expected to find the warders your slaves.

B. 20 (*enigmatically*). My dear Blanche, I can never speak of his conduct and attention as they deserve.

LADY WINDHAM. I knew it! What a nice, kind man! I like his face immensely, Colonel; and I can always read character. [*Exit warder, at motion of Governor.*] But why don't you speak, Charlie. Aren't you pleased to see us? I want you to come at once to Scotland, for a week's holiday.

B. 20 (*in his Parliamentary style*). Ah! the mountains and moorlands, that bring health and hope to the jaded spirit! And what shall I leave behind me—*here!* What broken spirits and hopeless lives! No, no! let me serve my time, like the rest.

LADY WINDHAM (*aside to the Governor*). Oh, don't mind him, please! It's only his way of speaking—his Parliamentary manner, you know.

THE GOVERNOR (*who seems to be divided between wounded pride at the slight to his discipline and sensibility to Lady Windham's attractions*). It's the discipline of this prison I am thinking of, Lady Windham.

MR. GRAVELY. And I am thinking of the imminent scandal at the Home Office.

B. 20.   I have treated you very badly, Colonel Stark. I apologise with all my heart for playing this trick upon you. But if you knew my motives for what I have done, I am sure you would pardon me.

THE GOVERNOR.   There is only one person who can pardon you, Sir Charles, and that is the Home Secretary— yourself. You will need a free pardon from him before you can be discharged from prison.

MR. GRAVELY.   I have provided for that, Colonel Stark. (*Producing a paper.*) I have brought the form with me for Sir Charles to sign. But the whole proceeding is in the highest degree anomalous. I can scarcely bring myself to be a party to it.

B. 20 (*deferentially*).   Yes, I owe you, too, an apology, Gravely, in view of your position at the Home Office. (*Becoming Parliamentary.*) It was thoughtless of me to forget that a Permanent Official is not, like a Home Secretary, a comparatively irresponsible individual—a mere passenger, so to speak, who comes and goes with his party—but the pilot who steers the ship and has the deepest interest in its welfare.

LADY WINDHAM.   Why, Charlie, I declare your speaking has improved since you've been in prison! You *will* forgive him, Colonel, won't you? And you, Mr. Gravely?

THE GOVERNOR.   Certainly, Lady Windham, certainly. But may I ask the Home Secretary how he came into this place? I trust no other members of the Government are "doing time" here, *incognito?*

MR. GRAVELY.   And *why* did you come here, Sir Charles? What reason could there be for so amazing an indiscretion?

B. 20.   You may well ask me those questions. Well, in the first place, I acted from conscientious motives, as I thought, to get a knowledge at first hand of what the prison system means, not to judges or juries, or lawyers, or gaolers, but to the prisoners themselves. And secondly, I got in here by the connivance of an officer who substituted me, between the police-court and the prison gate, for the real offender—a man who had defrauded a railway company of some trifling sum.

[*The Governor shrugs his shoulders: Mr. Gravely holds up his hands in silent despair.*]

LADY WINDHAM.   It was splendid of you, Charlie! The most romantic thing you've ever done, by far!

MR. GRAVELY.   The most improper thing any Home Secretary has ever done, in my experience—and I've known six Ministries.

THE GOVERNOR.   And the result of your investigations, Sir Charles?

B. 20.   Ah, the result! Well, however tamely the experiment has ended—and you think me a fool, I know—I have learnt, by personal experience, that the system of solitary confinement, the throwing back of the sinner's mind on itself, as Mr. Prim expresses it, is an inhuman absurdity, which defeats its own purpose, and sends the prisoner out from his cell a worse man than he entered it.

LADY WINDHAM (*meditatively*).   Are *you* worse, Charlie?

B. 20.   If I am not so, my dear Blanche, it is only because I have not been long enough in this beautifully clean little cell that you so much admire—this whited sepulchre, as I should call it rather.

MR. GRAVELY.   Pshaw, Sir Charles! You talk like the Humanitarian League. You know the prisons are arranged in full accordance with the advice of scientific experts, on the very best principles.

B. 20.   Principles? Criminological principles you mean, I suppose! All I say to you, Gravely, is, *try it.* You will find very quickly that experience and experts differ. And there is a still worse barbarity behind the scenes. I heard a cry not ten minutes before you entered—so revolting in its hideousness that, if it could be but once reproduced in the House of Commons, I believe the use of the lash would be then and there prohibited. How can you, Colonel Stark, kindhearted man that you are, give the order for such a punishment?

THE GOVERNOR.   You forget, sir, that the order, before it could be carried out, had to be sanctioned by the Department over which you preside.

MR. GRAVELY.   It was signed by the Under Secretary, in your absence, Sir Charles. Colonel Stark was perfectly in order.

B. 20.   That is just the mischief of it. Everyone is perfectly in order, yet no one is personally responsible, and so the thing goes on. Well, it is useless for me to talk of it; and the governor, I know, thinks me a mere babbler. We shall see. But now, what am I to do, Gravely, to get out of prison? I have to pardon myself, have I not? Please instruct me—as usual.

[*They confer over the papers brought by Gravely.*]

LADY WINDHAM (*apart to Governor*).   I suppose the man who was flogged was a *very* wicked character?

THE GOVERNOR.   Insubordination, madam. We have to maintain discipline, you know.

LADY WINDHAM.   Of course, of course, Colonel. I do so sympathise with you. I have to punish my little boy sometimes for the same offence, and I feel it so dreadfully.

THE GOVERNOR. No doubt, madam. And does Sir Charles feel it equally?

LADY WINDHAM. Why no! That's the curious thing about it. He only laughs.

MR. GRAVELY *(interrupting)*. Look here, Colonel Stark, shall we get this pardon signed at once, and give our prisoner his discharge?

THE GOVERNOR. By all means. But not in this cell— you must come to my house for it. *(To Lady W.)* And after that I hope for the honour of your company to lunch.

LADY WINDHAM. You are very kind, colonel. But do, please, let the pardon be signed *here,* in the very place where my husband has spent his holiday. It is so much, much more romantic!

THE GOVERNOR. As you will, Lady Windham, as you will. Your wishes are commands in this matter. But at least permit Sir Charles to come to my rooms, to take off these prison togs and put his own clothes on again. We'll be back in five minutes, Mr. Gravely, if you'll prepare the documents.

[*Exeunt Governor and B. 20. Mr. Gravely busies himself in arranging the table and papers, while Lady Windham examines the cell.*]

LADY WINDHAM. I am glad to have a quiet look at Sir Charles's little hermitage. It does so remind me of Thoreau's hut at Walden. Mr. Gravely, do you agree with Sir Charles that prisons are uncomfortable?

MR. GRAVELY. On the contrary, Lady Windham, I think they are far too comfortable. If we go on letting the humanitarians have their way, the working-classes will be flocking into the gaols in preference to their own dwellings.

LADY WINDHAM. Really? Then perhaps that would

solve another problem that Sir Charles is interested in—the Housing of the Poor?

MR. GRAVELY (*smiling faintly*).   In a way it would, certainly, Lady Windham. But you see we want to set the rascally poor to *work;* not to make them comfortable at the public expense.

LADY WINDHAM (*sympathetically*).   I suppose these reforms of the prison system give a lot of trouble at the Home Office, Mr. Gravely?

MR. GRAVELY.   Oh, we don't think of *that,* Lady Windham. A Permanent Official never minds trouble. It is entirely on principle that we object to such changes. The criminal population must be kept in proper control.

THE WARDER (*opening the door*).   The Visiting Justice!

[*Enter Mr. Prim.*]

MR. PRIM (*staggered at the sight*).   What's this, warder? A lady and gentleman! Oh, visitors, I presume. I beg your pardon, I'm sure. I came to have another word with our poor friend here (*looking round in bewilderment*).

LADY WINDHAM.   Was it B. 20 you were looking for, sir? He's just gone out with the Governor, and will be back in a moment?

MR. PRIM.   I thank you, madam. I rejoice to see that respectable influences are being brought to bear on him. A strange character his!—with much of good, as well as of bad, in it.

MR. GRAVELY.   Ahem! I must tell you, sir, that this prisoner——

LADY WINDHAM (*interrupting*).   I can assure you, sir, that there is far, far more good than bad in the man. I know him better than anyone does.

214

MR. PRIM.   A woman's gracious influence may do much, very much, madam, to soften the sinner's heart, when a salutary discipline has already awakened it. Solitude, segregation, self-questioning, remorse—these are the ordained instruments for the reclamation of the offender——

[*Enter the Governor and Sir Charles Windham. The latter is faultlessly attired in frock-coat, &c.*]

THE GOVERNOR.   Aha, Mr. Prim! I'm glad you've found your way here again. We shall want you, presently, to witness a signature. But let me introduce you. This is Sir Charles Windham, the Home Secretary—Lady Windham—Mr. Gravely, of the Home Office.

SIR C. WINDHAM.   So you see the sinner clothed and in his right mind, Mr. Prim: thanks to Criminological Principles, of course! Segregation, solitude, self-questioning, &c., &c. Ha, Ha!—they've worked wonders in my case, have they not?

THE GOVERNOR.   I told you, Prim, I told you, that this sinner was very wide awake.

MR. PRIM (*distractedly*).   Oh, but, Sir Charles—I beg pardon, I am sure—not in your case, sir. The discipline I spoke of is for the sinner—not for the Home Secretary—oh, not for the Home Secretary; of course not.

SIR C. WINDHAM.   But where is the distinction, Mr. Prim? Who is, and who is not, the sinner? "There, but for the grace of God, goes John Bradford," you know. And if John Bradford, why not the Home Secretary also?

MR. PRIM (*recovering himself*).   True, sir, but the grace of God makes all the difference. I ought to have recognised it in your case, Sir Charles. I trust you will pardon the oversight.

SIR C. WINDHAM.   Well, you are not the first person,

Mr. Prim, who has recognised it more easily in the frock-coat than in the broad-arrow.

MR. GRAVELY.   At any rate I trust Mr. Prim will recognise the necessity of keeping this incident very strictly private.

MR. PRIM.   Rely on me, rely on me, Mr. Gravely.

THE GOVERNOR.   Well, gentlemen, shall we now proceed to business?

[*The Home Secretary sits down on the four-legged stool, at the table, facing audience; meantime a chair has been brought in by the Warder for Lady Windham. The rest stand round the table.*]

SIR C. WINDHAM (*critically and judicially, looking at the papers*).   I see, Gravely, that this document grants a free pardon to one George Tomkins, found guilty of defrauding a Railway Company of the sum of seven and sixpence.

LADY WINDHAM.   Oh, Charlie, I shall always call you Tomkins after this.

SIR C. WINDHAM.   Hush, my dear, hush!

MR. GRAVELY (*tartly*).   That is our regular form of procedure, Sir Charles. What is wrong with it?

SIR C. WINDHAM.   Oh, nothing, of course. But I am to understand, then, that I am releasing myself by pardoning another man for a crime which I didn't commit but he did? What do you make of that, Colonel? Is this in accordance with criminological principles, Mr. Prim?

THE GOVERNOR.   Principles or no principles, Sir Charles, you can't have your discharge until it is signed, that is certain.

LADY WINDHAM.   Oh, do be quick and sign it, Charlie! We have to start to-night for Scotland, you know. And please don't begin to be Parliamentary again or we shall miss the train.

SIR C. WINDHAM.   Very well, then. I must pardon myself for a crime of which I am wholly innocent.

MR. GRAVELY.   You don't understand our Home Office methods, Sir Charles. After a conviction we know of no such thing as "innocence." It is a case of prison or pardon—there is no other alternative. Besides (*smiling condescendingly*) you need have no scruple about giving yourself a free pardon for what you have *not* done, because we might, if we liked, keep you in prison for other things that you *have* done—such as conniving at a defeat of justice in the case of the said Tomkins.

SIR C. WINDHAM.   I have done that, certainly; but as I have not been charged with it, we could not consider it now.

MR. GRAVELY.   Oh, but indeed we could, Sir Charles, if we wished to keep you here. You don't know the official methods, you see. We take note at the Home Office of many offences besides those for which the prisoner has been convicted.

SIR C. WINDHAM (*impressed*).   Now do we, indeed, Gravely? That is very interesting. I had never heard of it before. So we take note of unproved guilt, it seems, but not of proved innocence! Well, as a Permanent Official, you must of course know best; but to me, as a mere Home Secretary, it seems an odd system.

MR. GRAVELY (*hurt*).   Surely, it is obvious, Sir Charles, that we ought not to let bad men out of prison sooner than we are obliged to.

MR. PRIM.   Certainly, certainly, Mr. Gravely. Not until they are awakened to a true sense of their position.

SIR C. WINDHAM (*cheerfully*).   Yes, those are the

criminological principles, Mr. Prim, no doubt. Well, as I *am* awakened to a sense of my position—by-the-bye *(half rising)* I find my position on this stool a very uncomfortable one. *(The Warder here rushes forward, and puts an armful of oakum as a cushion on the stool.)* Thank you, warder, thank you! As I *am* awakened, I say, to a sense of my position, and wish to get out of it with all speed, I hereby give Mr. Tomkins his discharge *(signs)*.

MR. GRAVELY.   Now for the witnesses. Mr. Prim, will you kindly act as one? I am the other. *(They sign.)* There, Governor! *(Handing him the paper.)*

THE GOVERNOR.   I congratulate you, Sir Charles! We must try to make you more comfortable on your next holiday visit.

SIR C. WINDHAM.   Don't be afraid, Colonel. I shall not trouble you again. I shall leave Mr. Tomkins to pick his own oakum next time.

LADY WINDHAM.   Oh, Charlie, do tell us something of that Tomkins. What did he look like when you changed places with him? Was he very grateful?

SIR C. WINDHAM.   Grateful! Not the least little bit. He stood still, as if dazed, for a moment or two; then bolted off, round a corner, without once looking back.

MR. GRAVELY.   And doubtless he has broken the law again by now. To play these pranks with the course of justice is to put a premium on crime.

SIR C. WINDHAM.   Yes, I must remorsefully admit that, with recidivism on the increase *(pauses, seeing Gravely's eye on him)*—it *is* on the increase, isn't it Gravely?

MR. GRAVELY.   It is, Sir Charles—owing to humanitarian interference with the wholesome rigours of imprisonment.

MR. PRIM.   Very true, Mr. Gravely, very true!

SIR C. WINDHAM (*continuing*).   With recidivism on the increase, it is of course possible that Mr. Tomkins may once more offend against the law. In that case I can only hope he will be a more satisfactory prisoner than I have been. (*Rising.*) I thank you, gentlemen, for the patience and consideration you have shown to me as B. 20. And now, Colonel Stark, we are ready to accompany you to your house.

THE GOVERNOR (*to Lady W., offering his arm*).   May I have the pleasure, Lady Windham?

LADY WINDHAM.   Oh, thank you, Colonel! What a treat you have given us! I *do* so like the romance of prison life. (*Looking back.*) I shall often think of Sir Charles's little hermitage. It's a perfect picture.

[*Exeunt Governor and Lady W., Mr. Prim and Mr. Gravely stand waiting for Sir C. Windham to follow. The Warder, all bows and smirks, stands by the door.*]

SIR C. WINDHAM.   So this is the end of "my prisons." (*To the Warder.*) Good bye, Warder; and when next some poor devil of a prisoner pretends to be the Home Secretary—or even the Archbishop—don't be too hard on him! Such unlikely things do sometimes happen, you see! (*Gives him money.*)

THE WARDER (*with obsequious bows*).   Oh, thank you, sir, thank you kindly, I'm sure. I'm sorry if I was rough on you, sir; but, if you'll excuse me saying it, you was a bit aggravating—indeed you was, sir. Such a power of talk, and me not knowing that you were a gentleman from Parliament, sir——

MR. GRAVELY (*interrupting*).   Shall we be going, Sir Charles? The sooner this incident is closed and forgotten, the better.

SIR C. WINDHAM.   One more farewell, Gravely, and I have done. In yonder cell *(pointing to the back wall)* is an unknown fellow-prisoner, to whom I would speak a word of cheer before I leave. Now, under the circumstances, what would you say to him, Gravely? And you, Mr. Prim?

MR. GRAVELY.   Say? Of course say nothing, Sir Charles. Such clandestine communication, on your part, would be doubly improper.

MR. PRIM.   I agree with Mr. Gravely, sir, that it would be most indecorous to hold such converse through the prison wall, however desirable it might be to direct the sinner's mind to a sense of its sinfulness.

SIR C. WINDHAM.   Ah, those are *your* criminological principles, Mr. Prim; mine are different. *(Becoming Parliamentary.)* I prefer to send a message of hope and brightness, which shall draw out the prisoner's thoughts as flowers are drawn towards the sun, as—*(pauses disconcerted on seeing that Lady W., with the Governor behind her, has returned to the door, and is watching him reproachfully).* Yes, yes, Blanche, I'm coming; in a moment.

LADY WINDHAM.   Oh, Charlie! You're being Parliamentary again, I declare, and you said you'd finished. We shall miss our train to a certainty. Do bring him along, Mr. Gravely; please!

[*Exeunt Lady W. and the Governor.*]

MR. GRAVELY.   Yes, come, Sir Charles; do.

SIR C. WINDHAM.   One moment, gentlemen! *(Goes to back wall, and gives a series of slow, measured taps.)*

MR. GRAVELY.   What! The gaol-bird's signal code! Has it come to that, Sir Charles?

SIR C. WINDHAM *(repeating the taps).*   Yes, Gravely. I too have graduated in Criminological Principles, you see. I came here a mere ignoramus in prison matters. I go out a Criminologist.

A VOICE (*faintly*).   Hullo, mate! Is that you? What's the news?

SIR C. WINDHAM (*in slow clear tones, using his hands as a speaking-trumpet*).   Buck up, my lad! buck up! It won't last for ever!

MR. GRAVELY AND MR. PRIM.   Sir Charles! Sir Charles! Restrain yourself!

THE VOICE.   Ay, ay, lad! Buck up, buck up! It won't last for ever!

[*Exit Sir C. Windham hastily, leaving the Warder gaping and grinning by the door, while Mr. Gravely and Mr. Prim stand aghast, in pious horror, with eyes and hands uplifted.*]

Index

223

R2